On Behalf of a Grateful Nation

Photography by
Tara Brundick & Patricia Brundick

This book is dedicated

to all the men and women

in the Armed Forces and their families.

Publisher: Tara Brundick
Editor Designer: Tara Brundick
Associate Editor: Patricia Brundick
All photos by: Tara Brundick and Patricia Brundick

ISBN 978-0-6151-5244-8

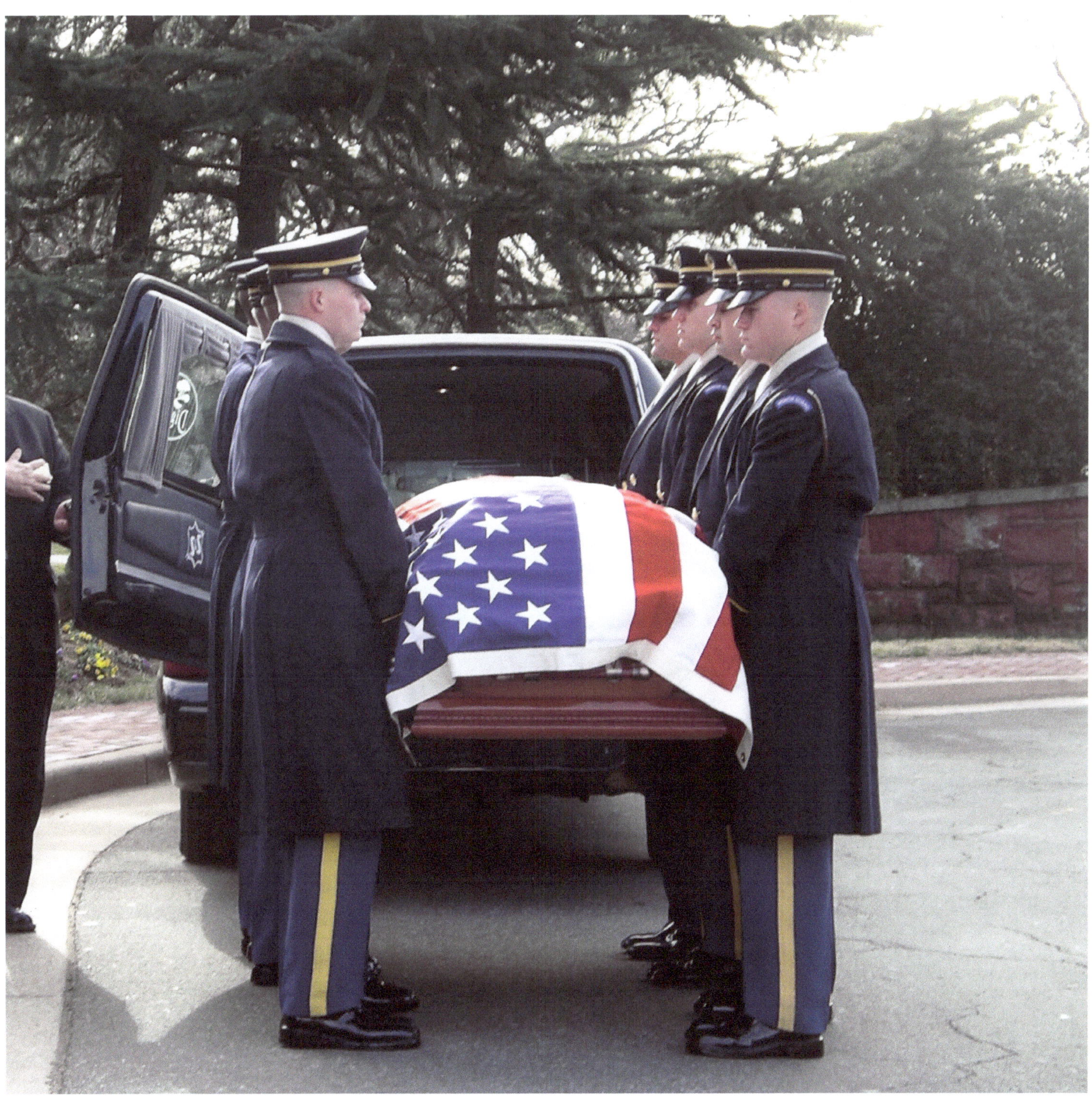

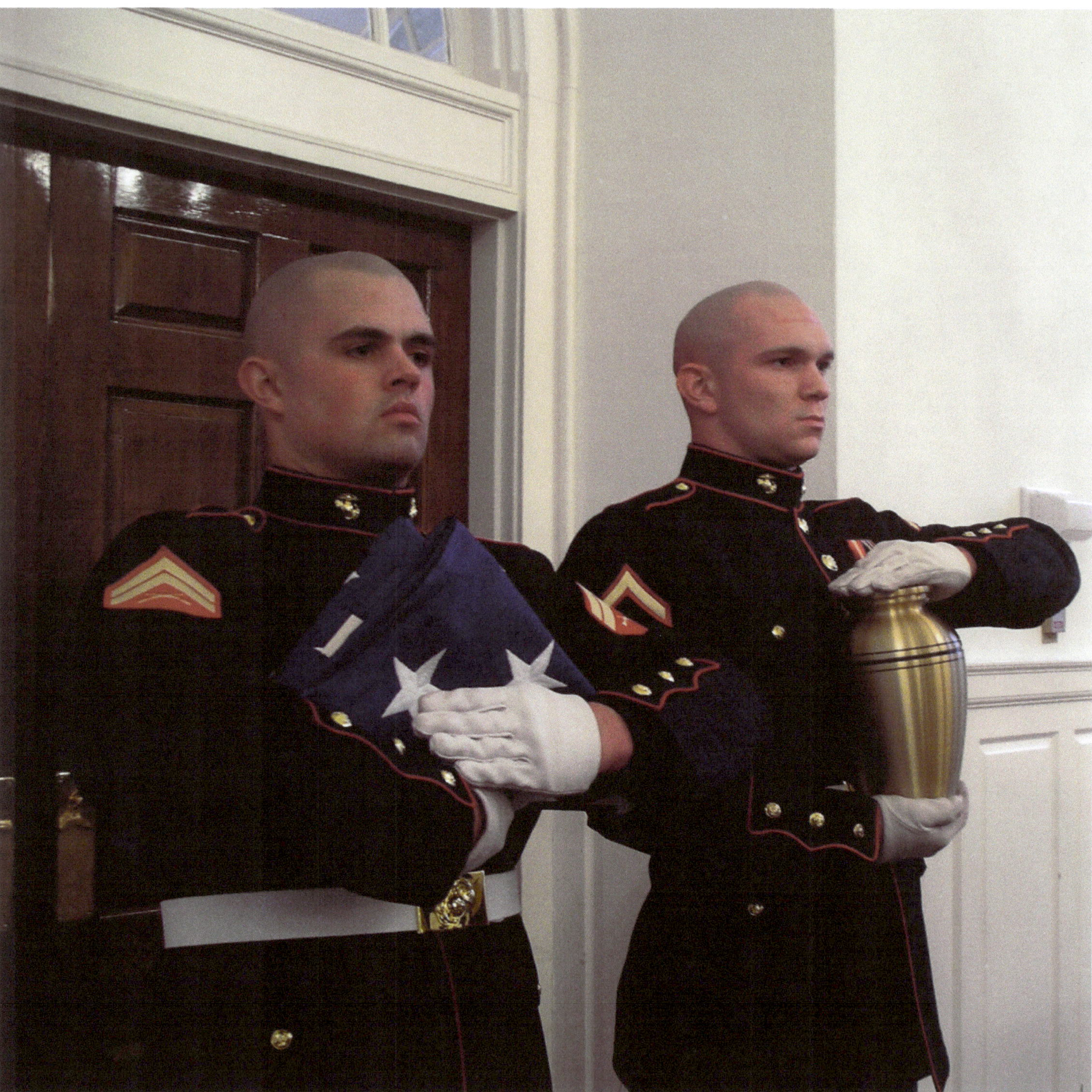

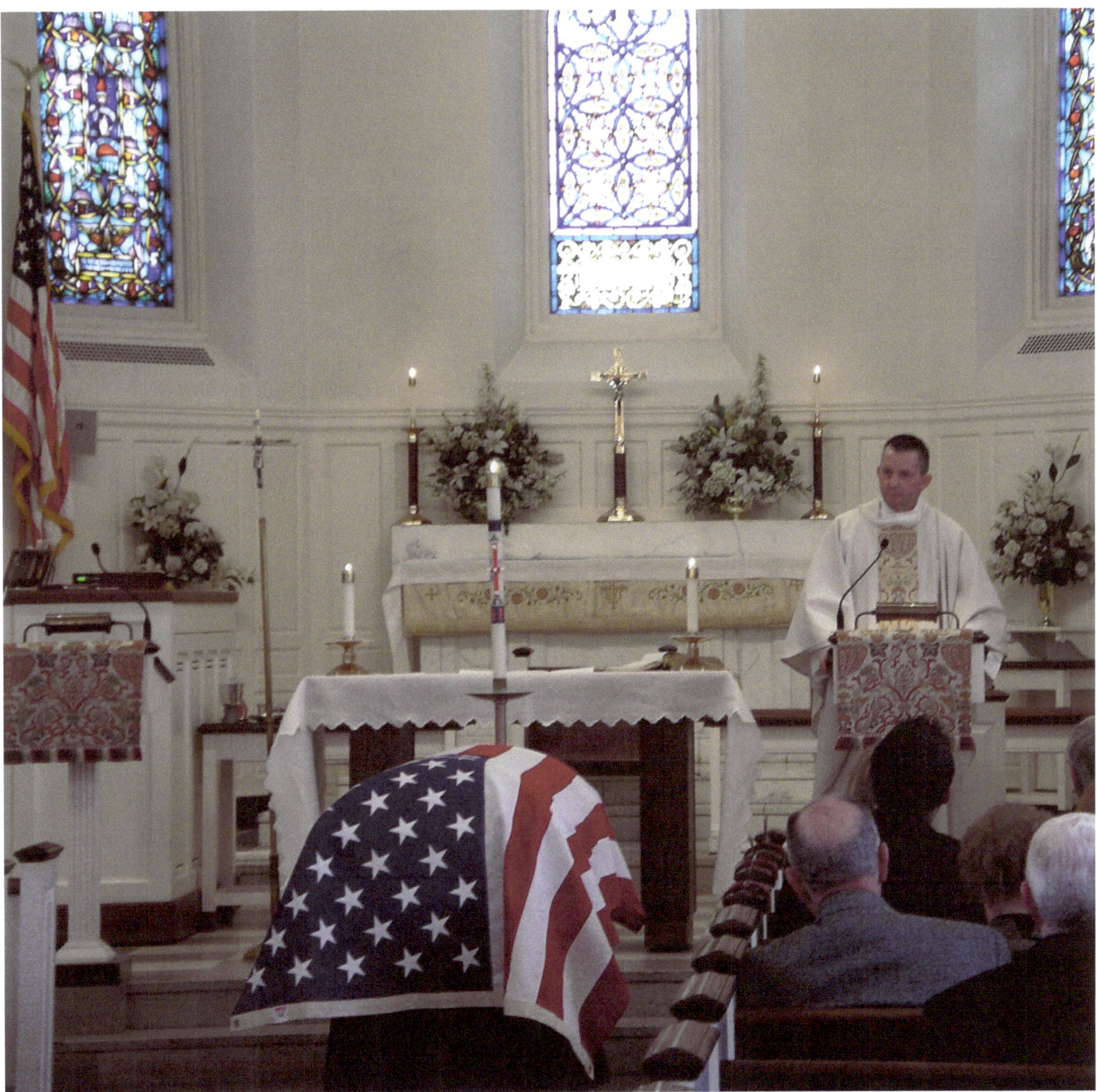

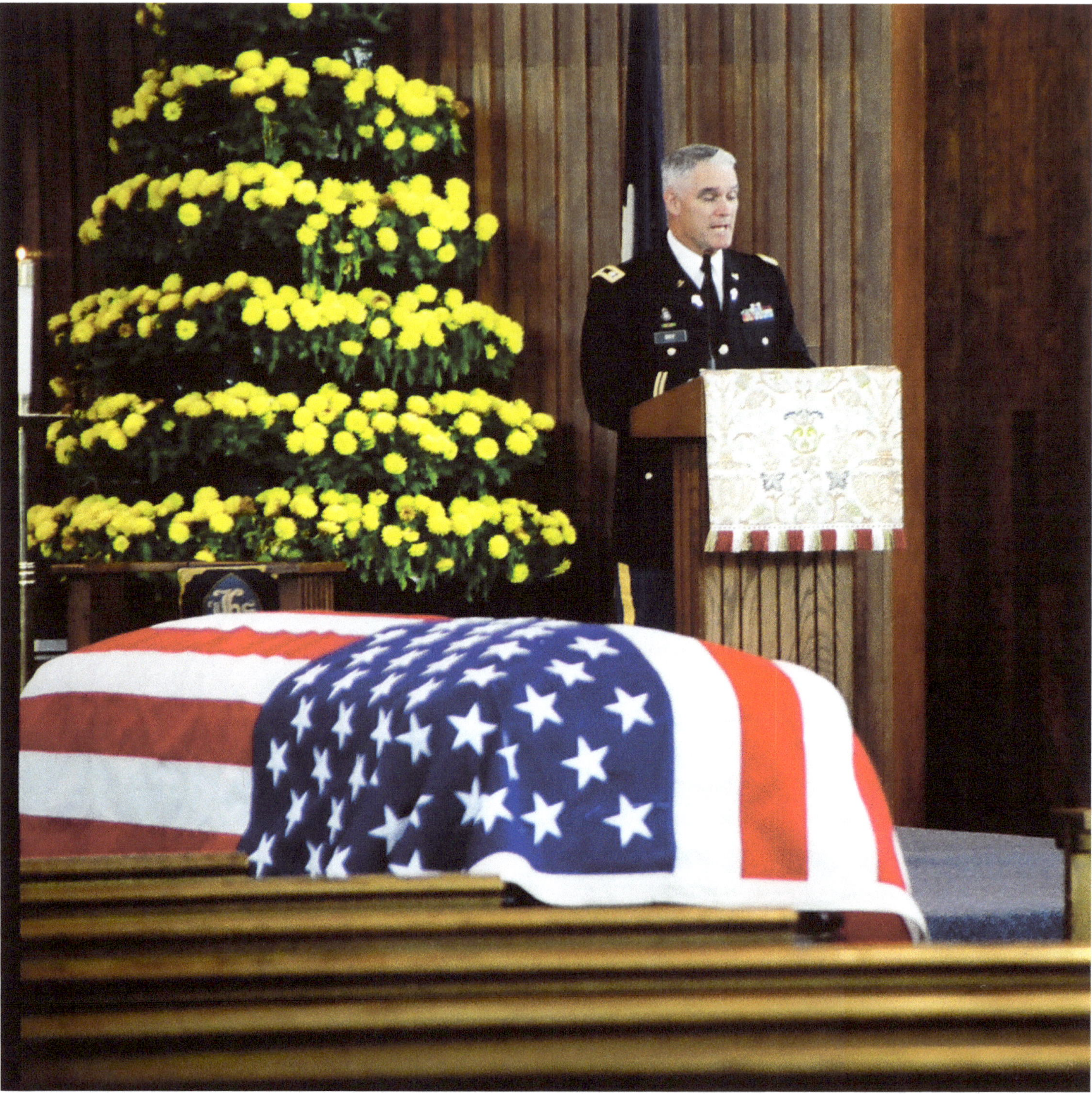

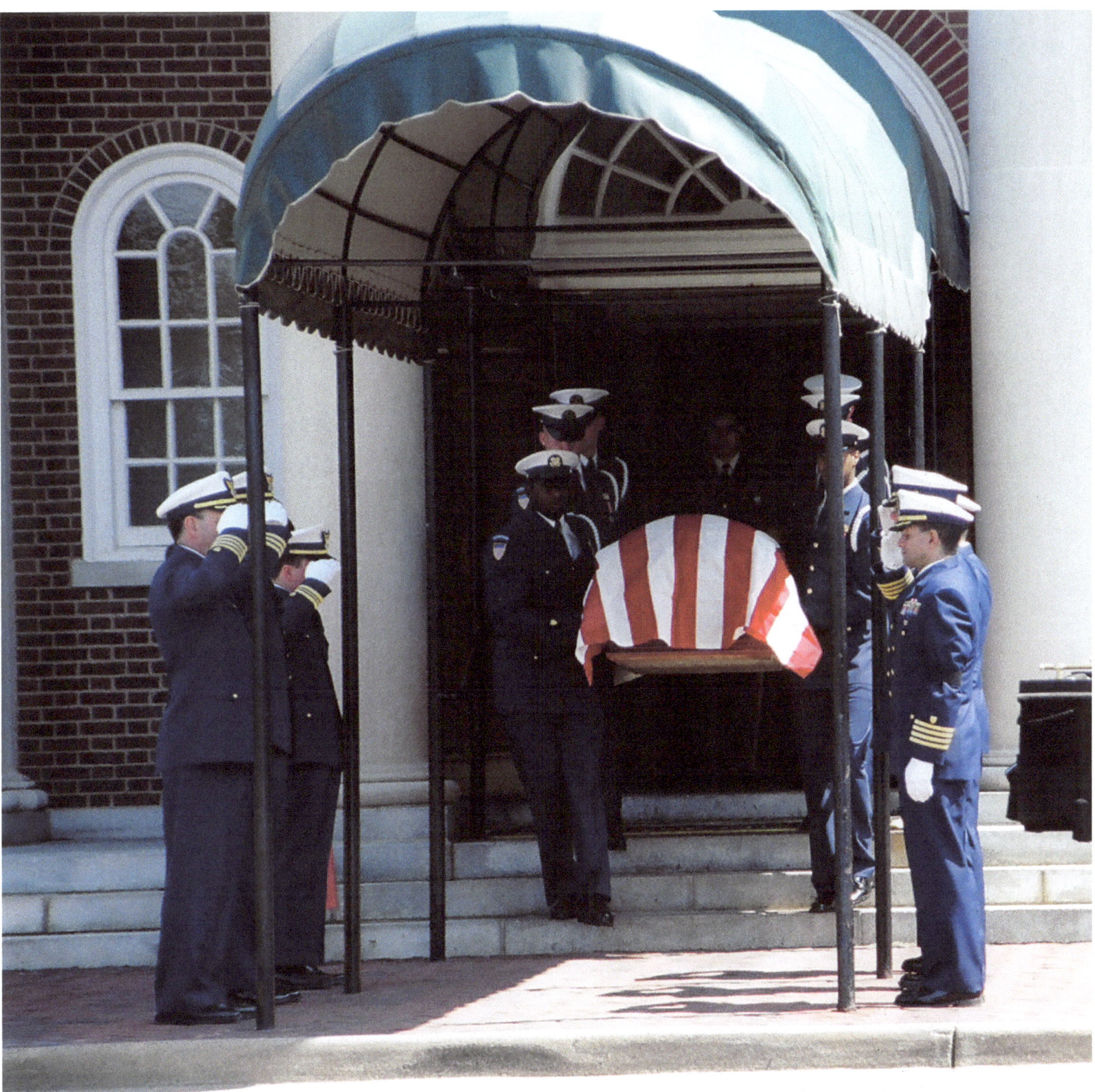

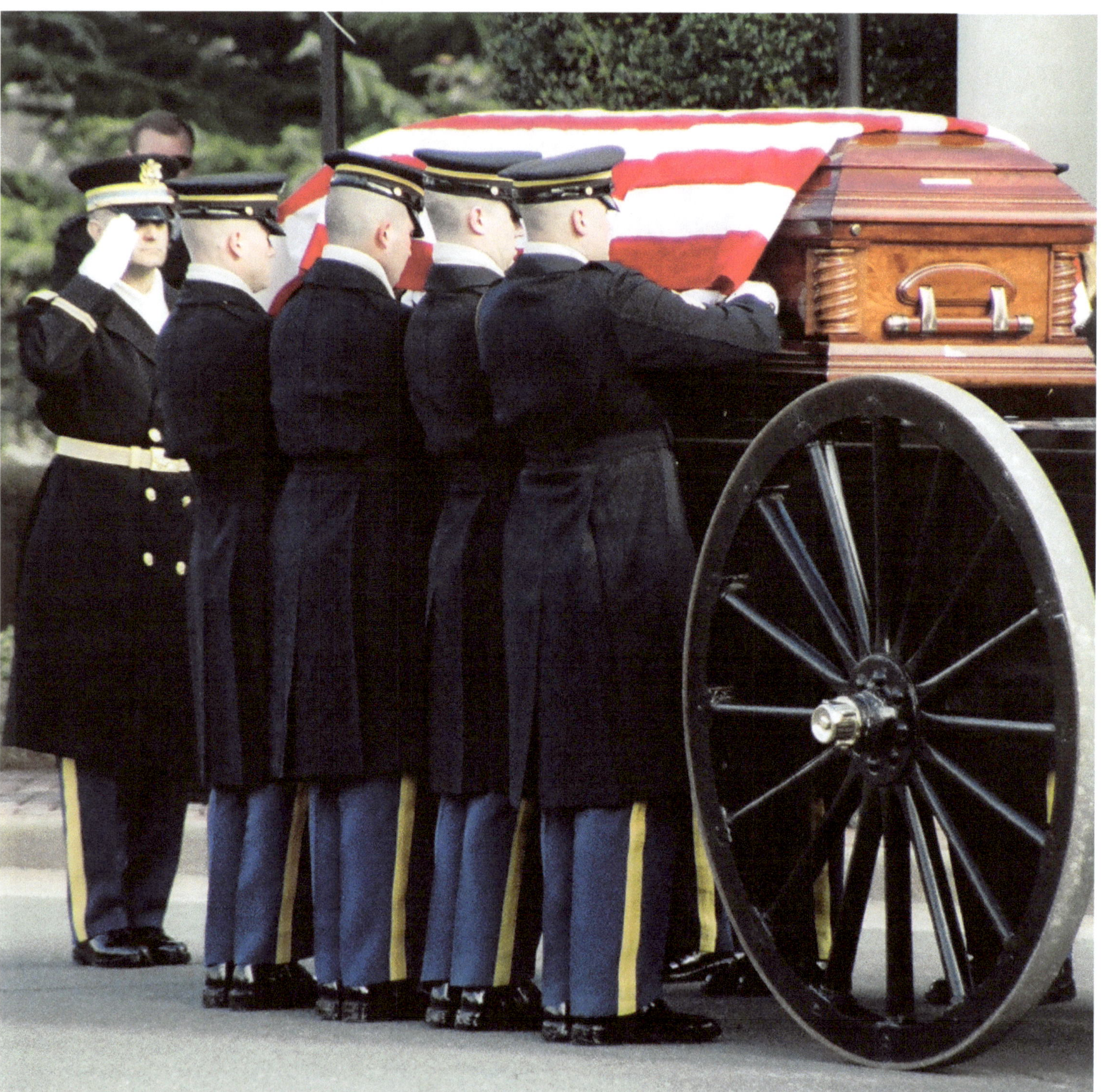

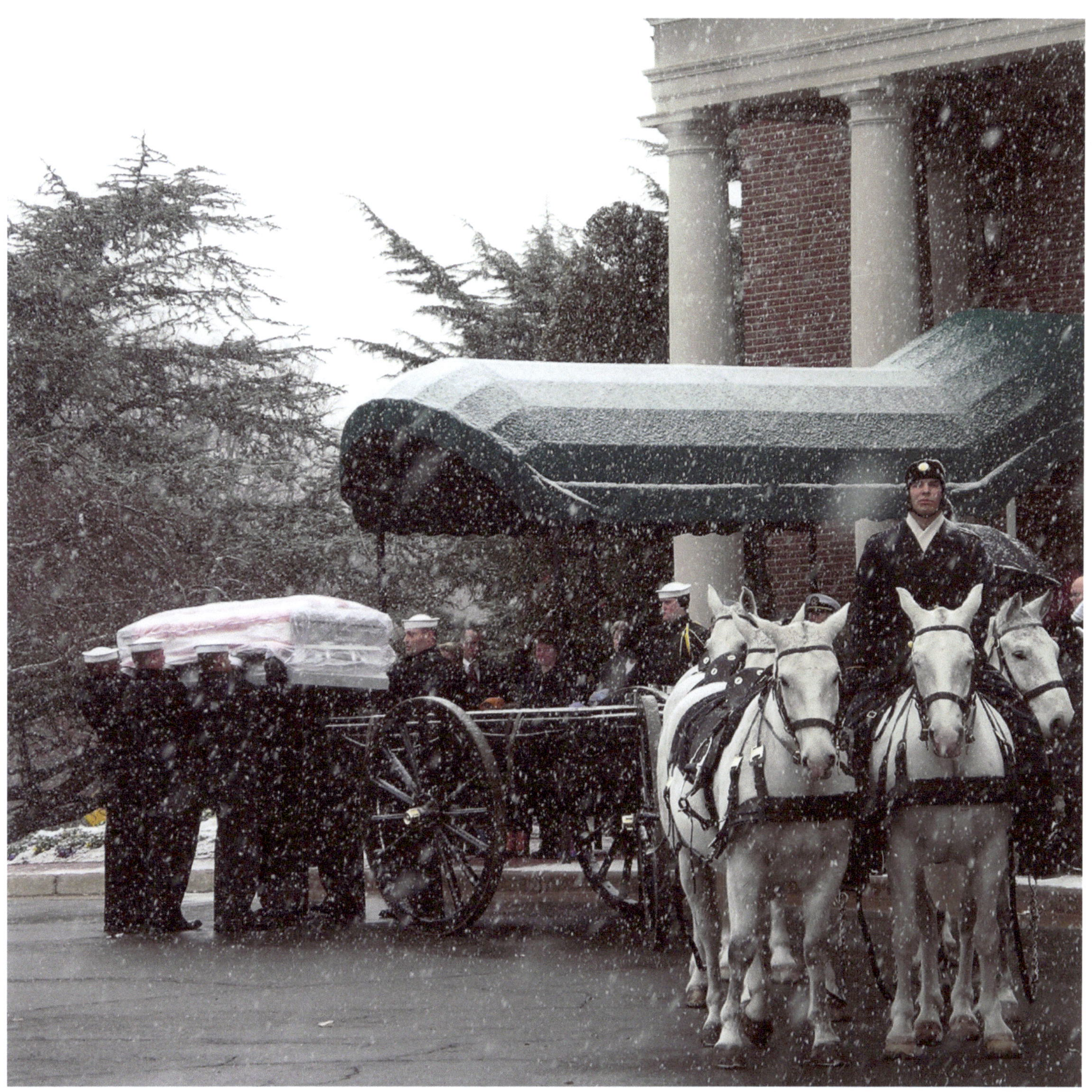

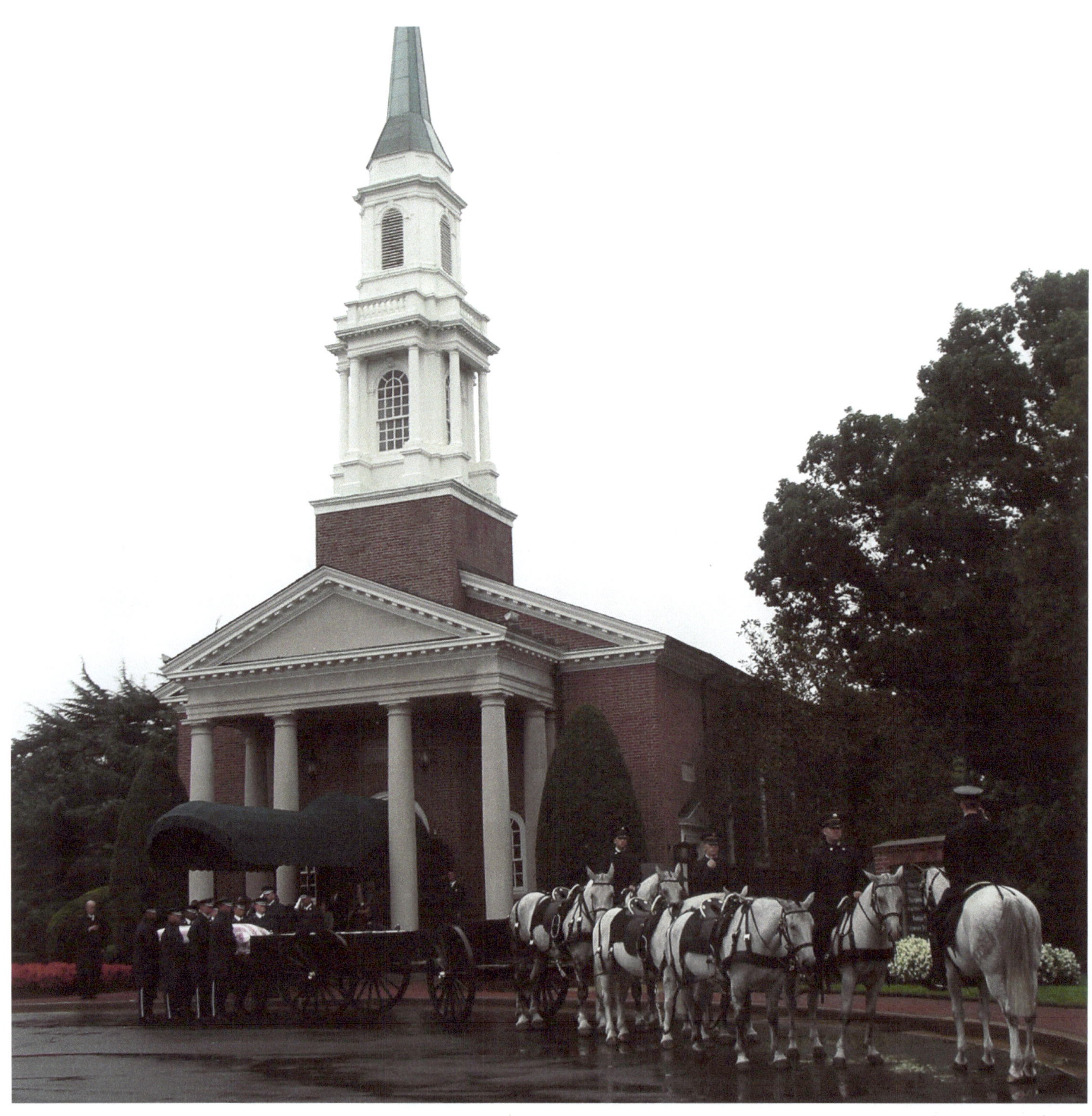

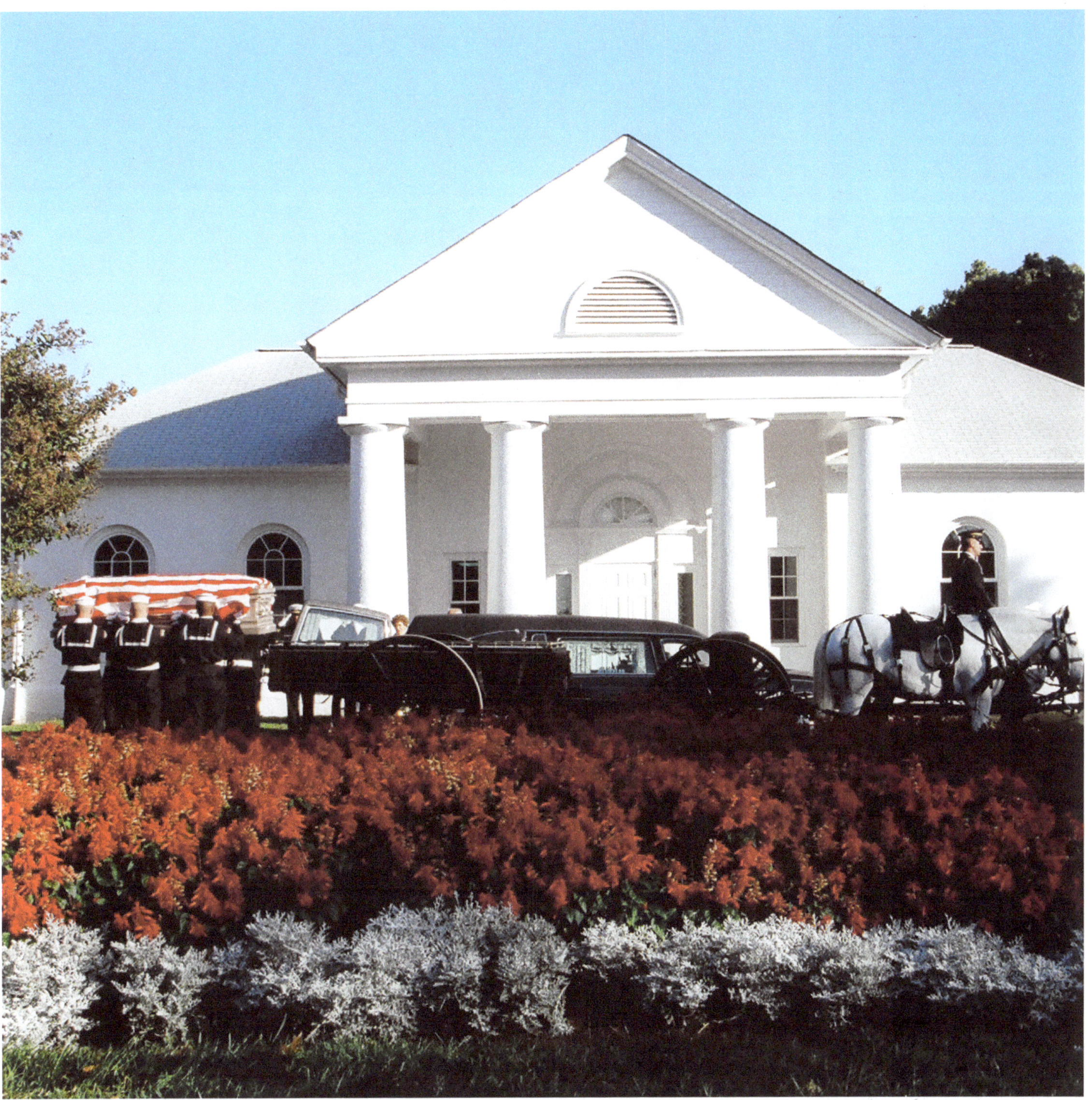

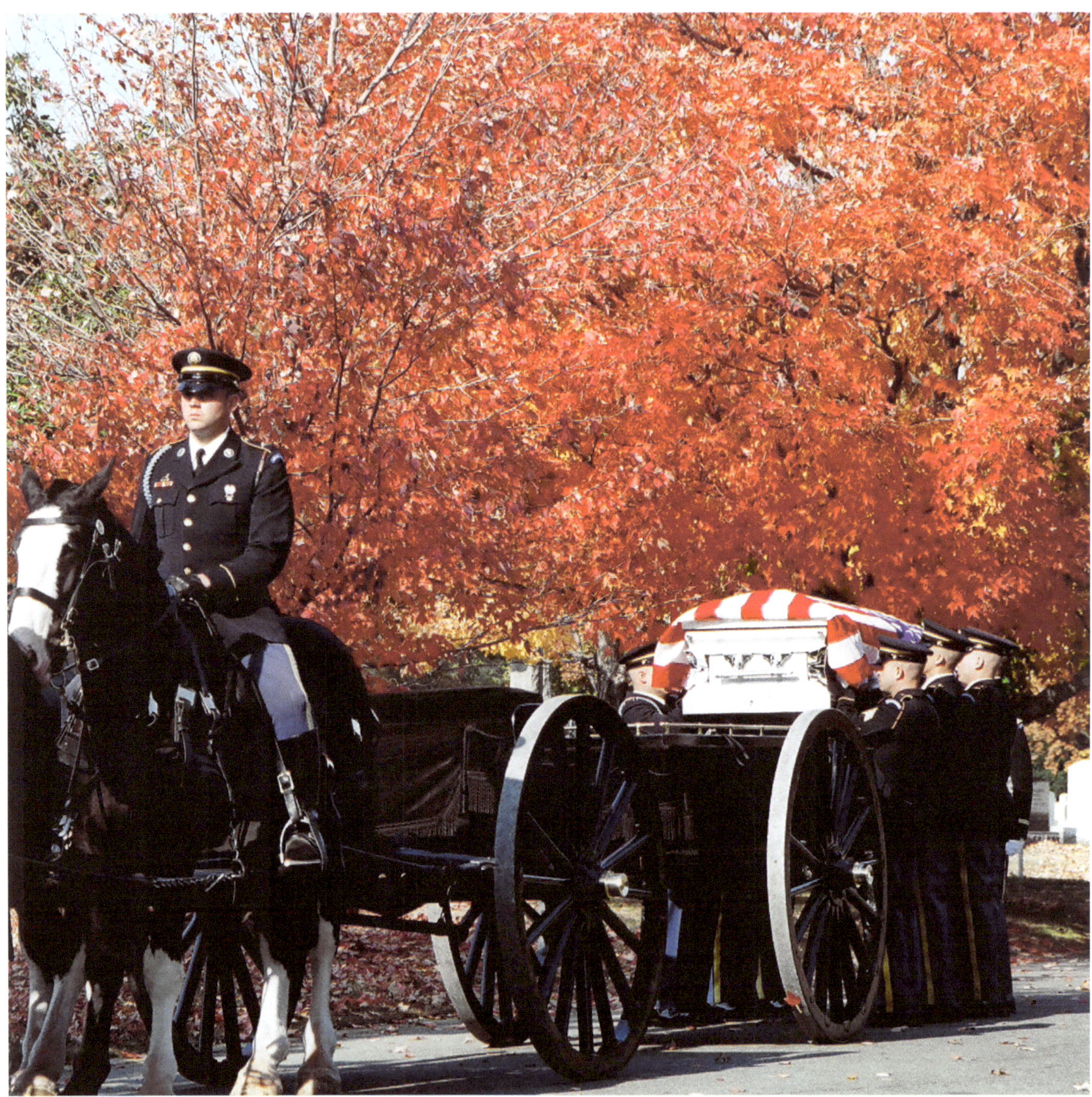

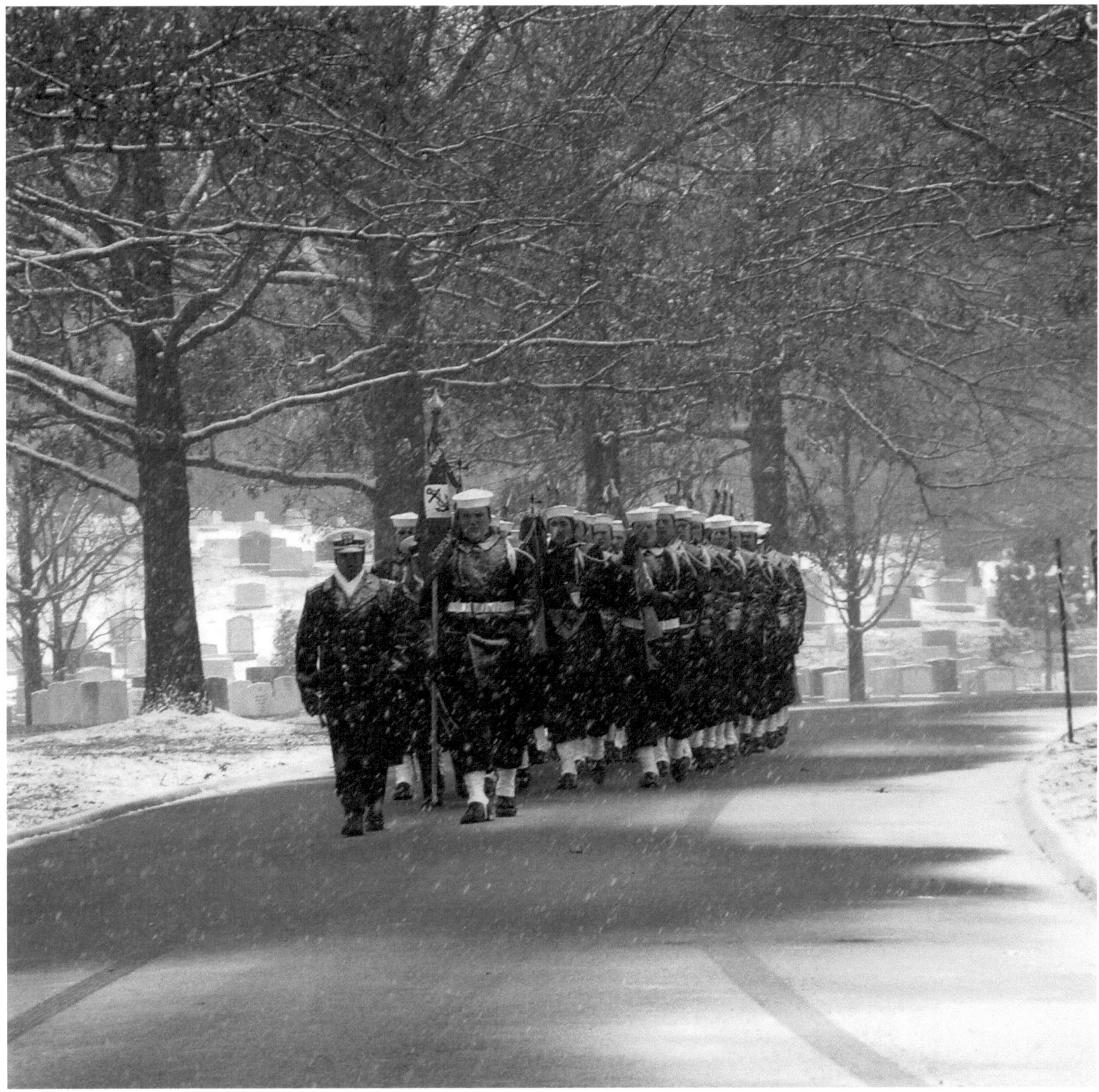

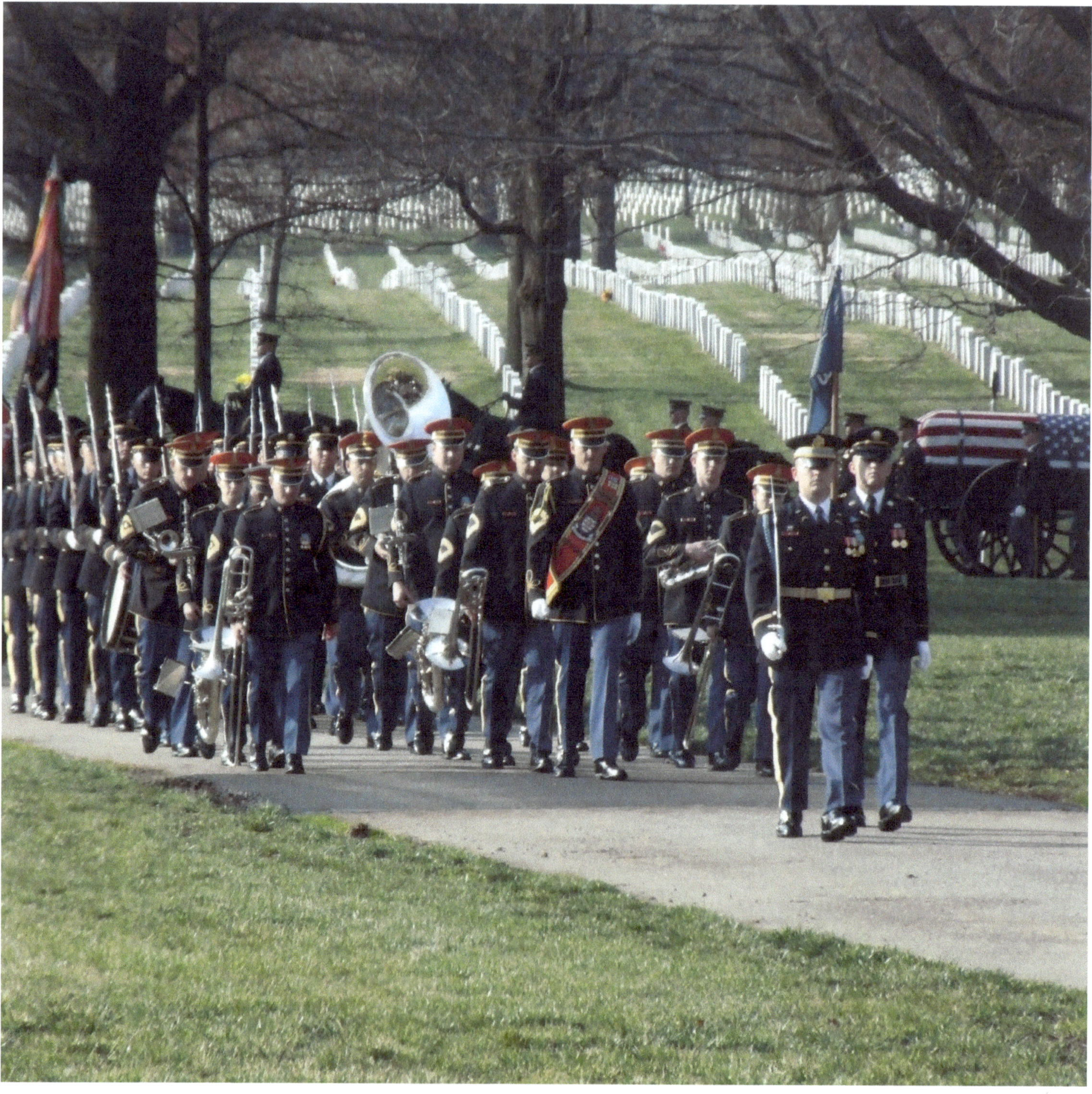

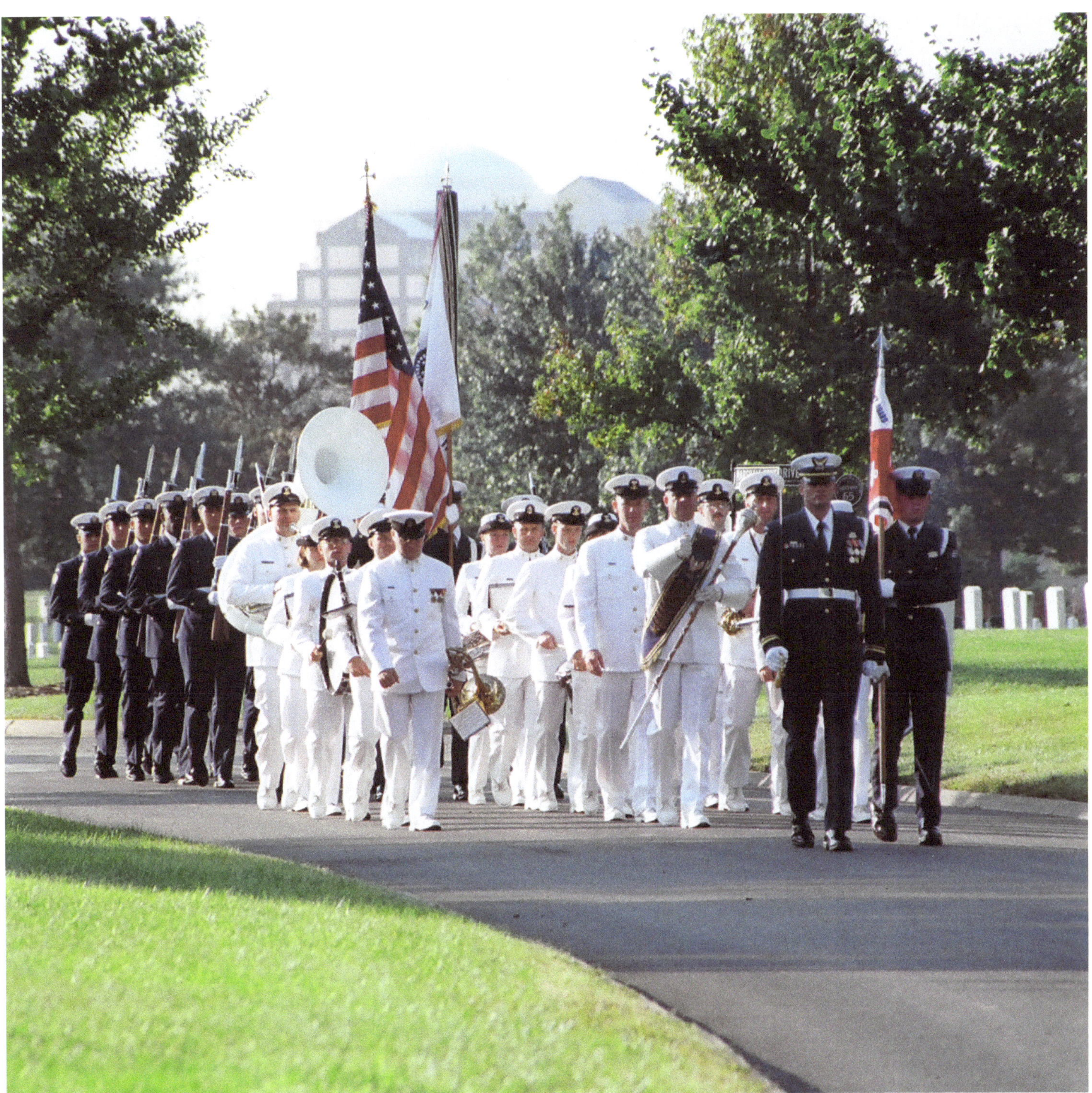

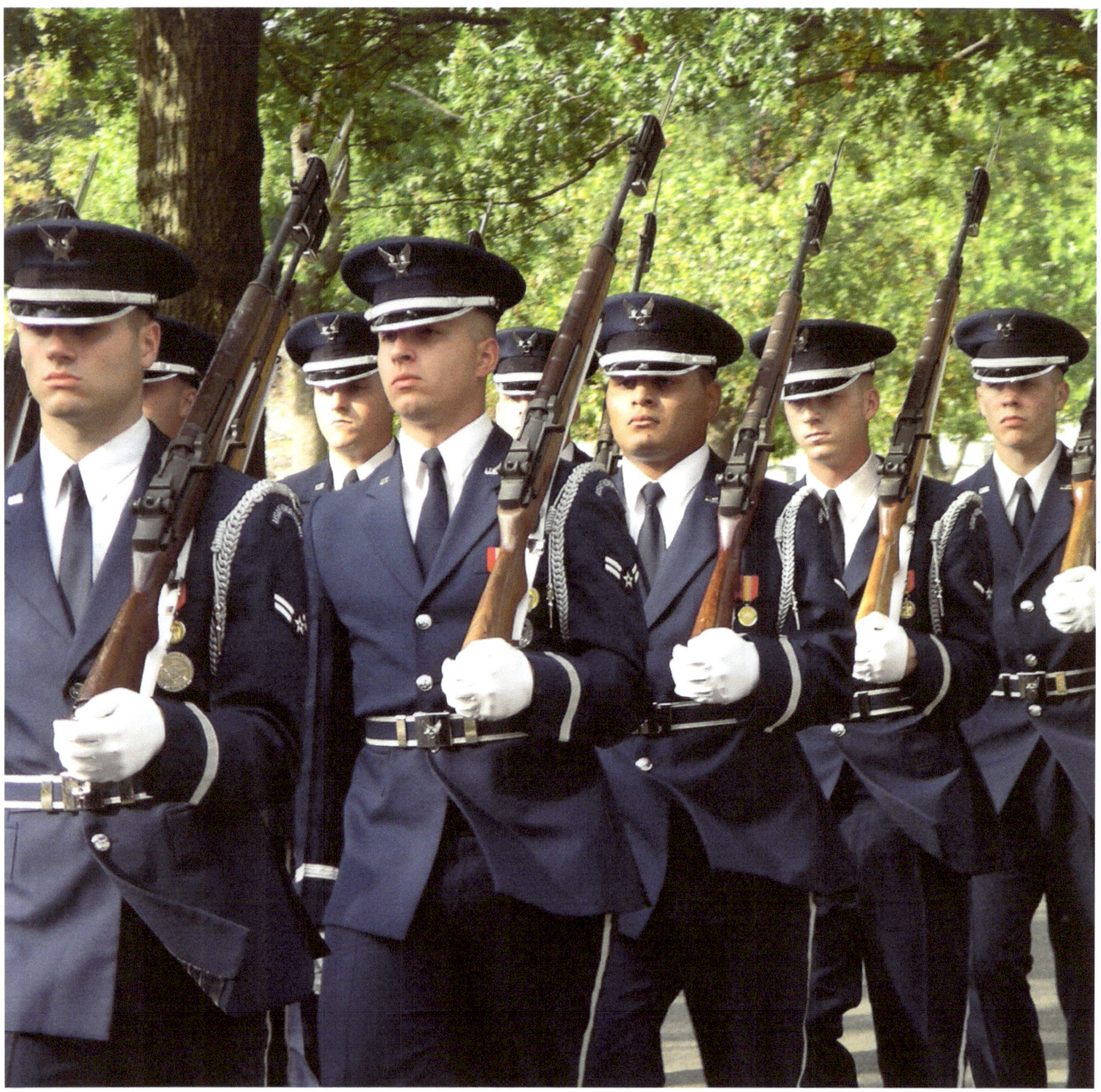

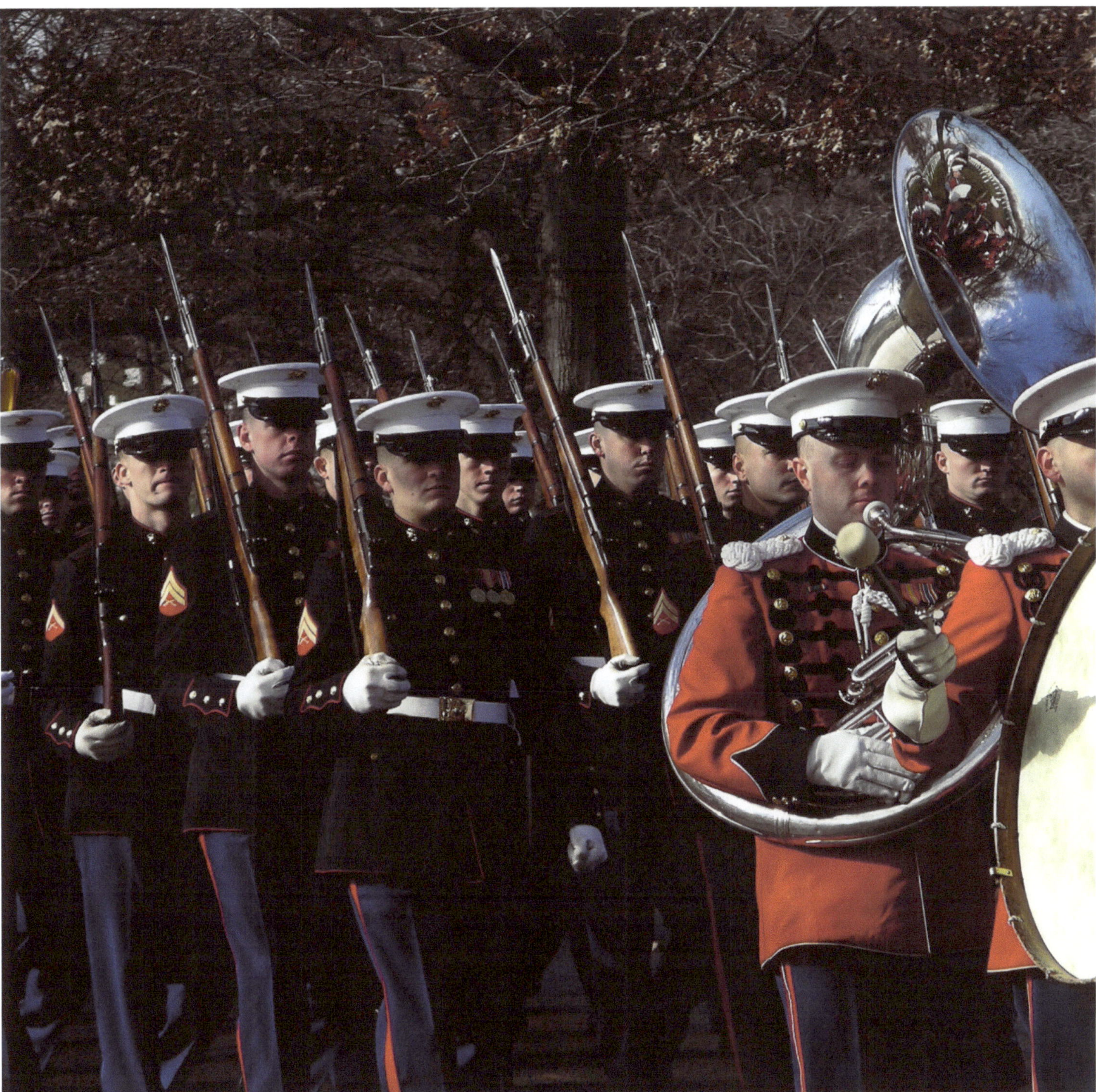

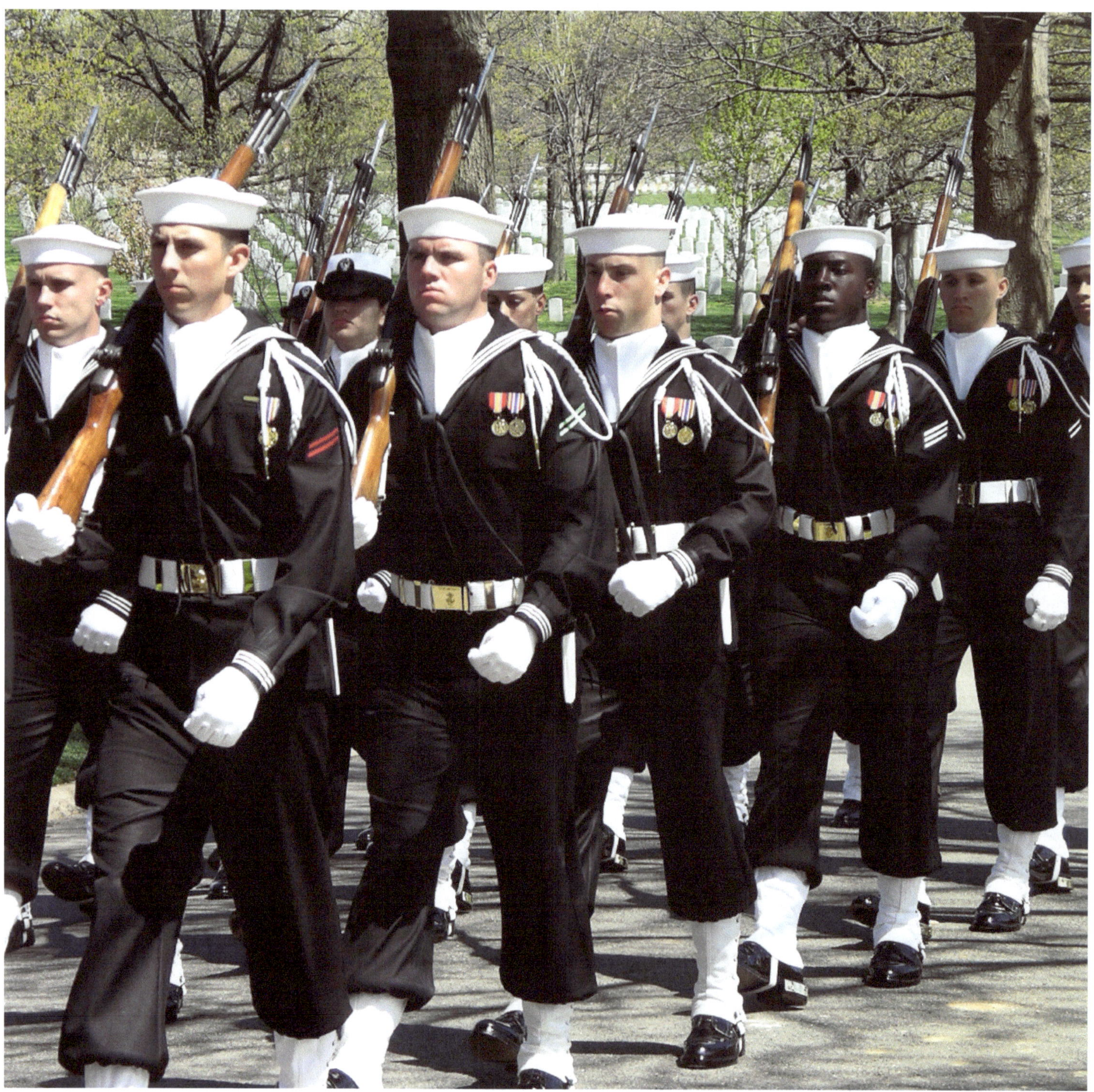

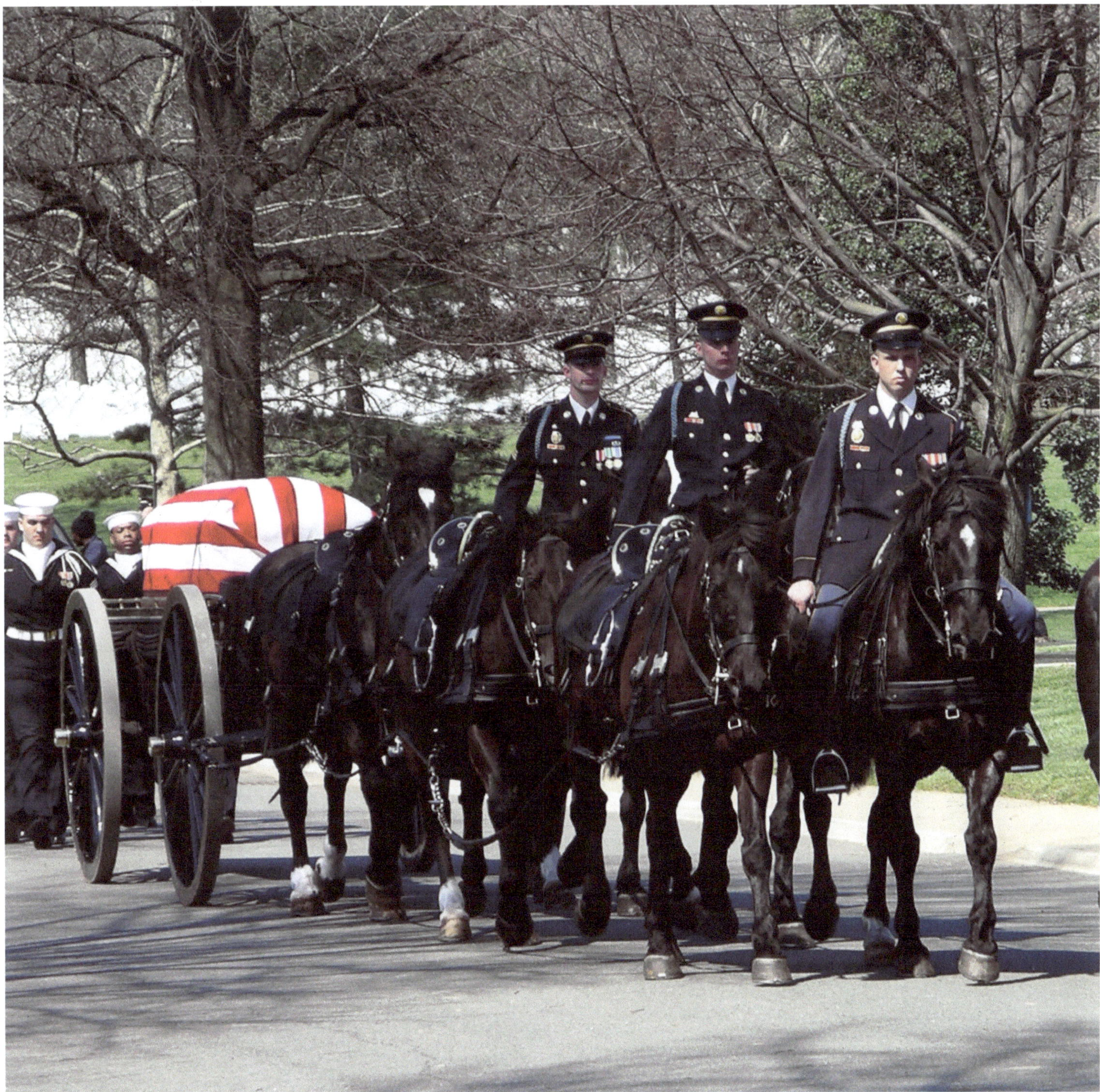

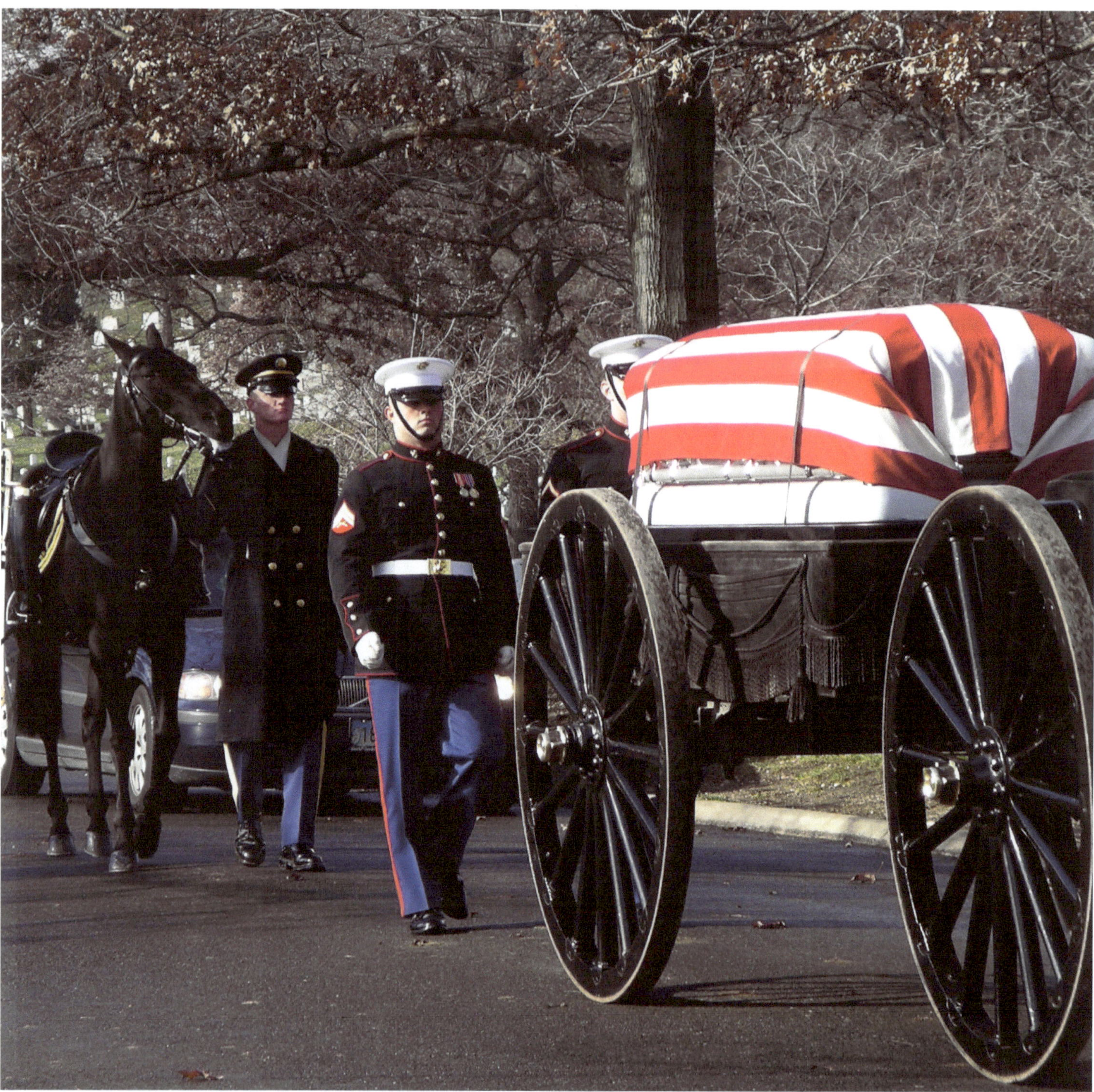

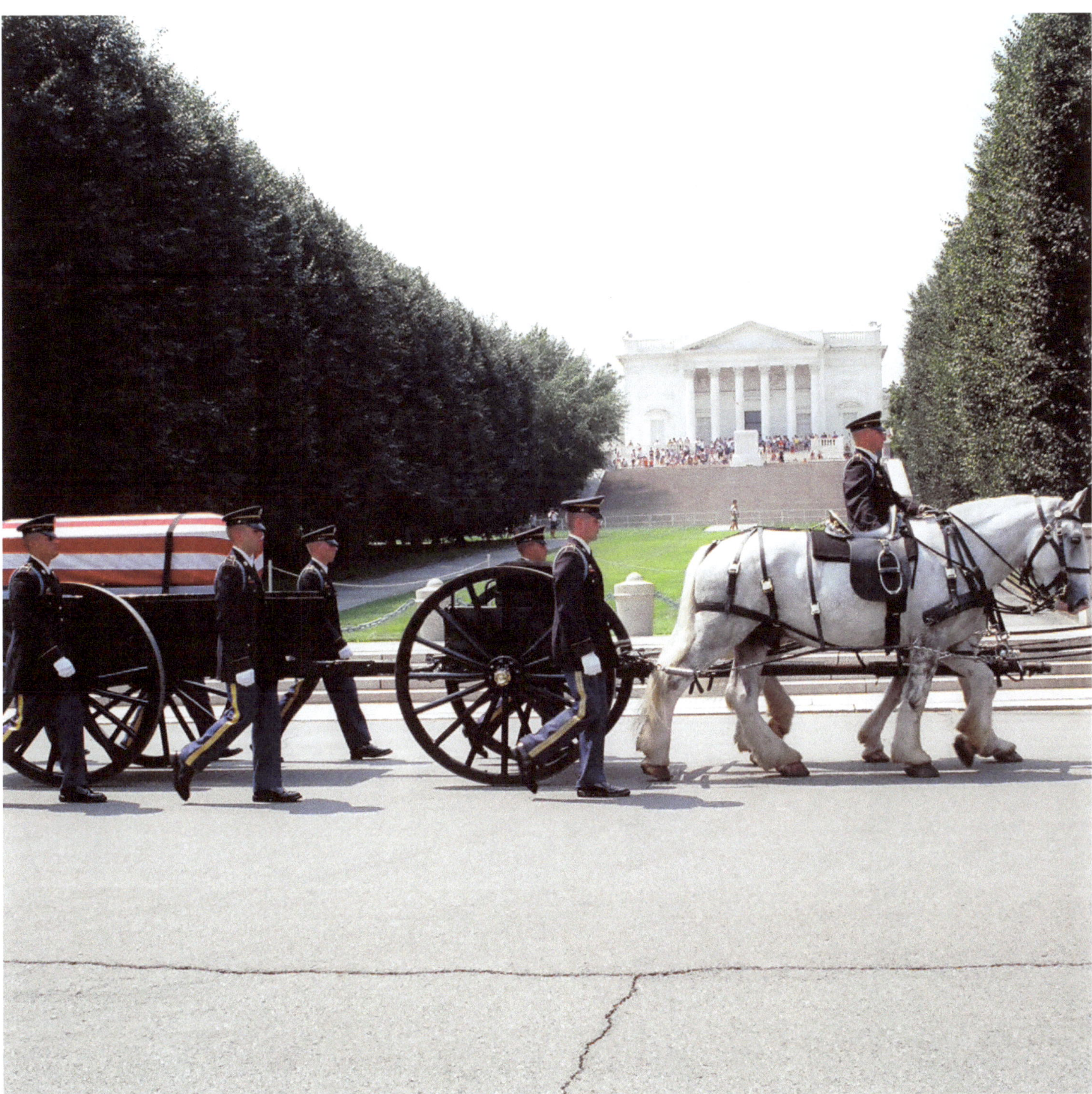

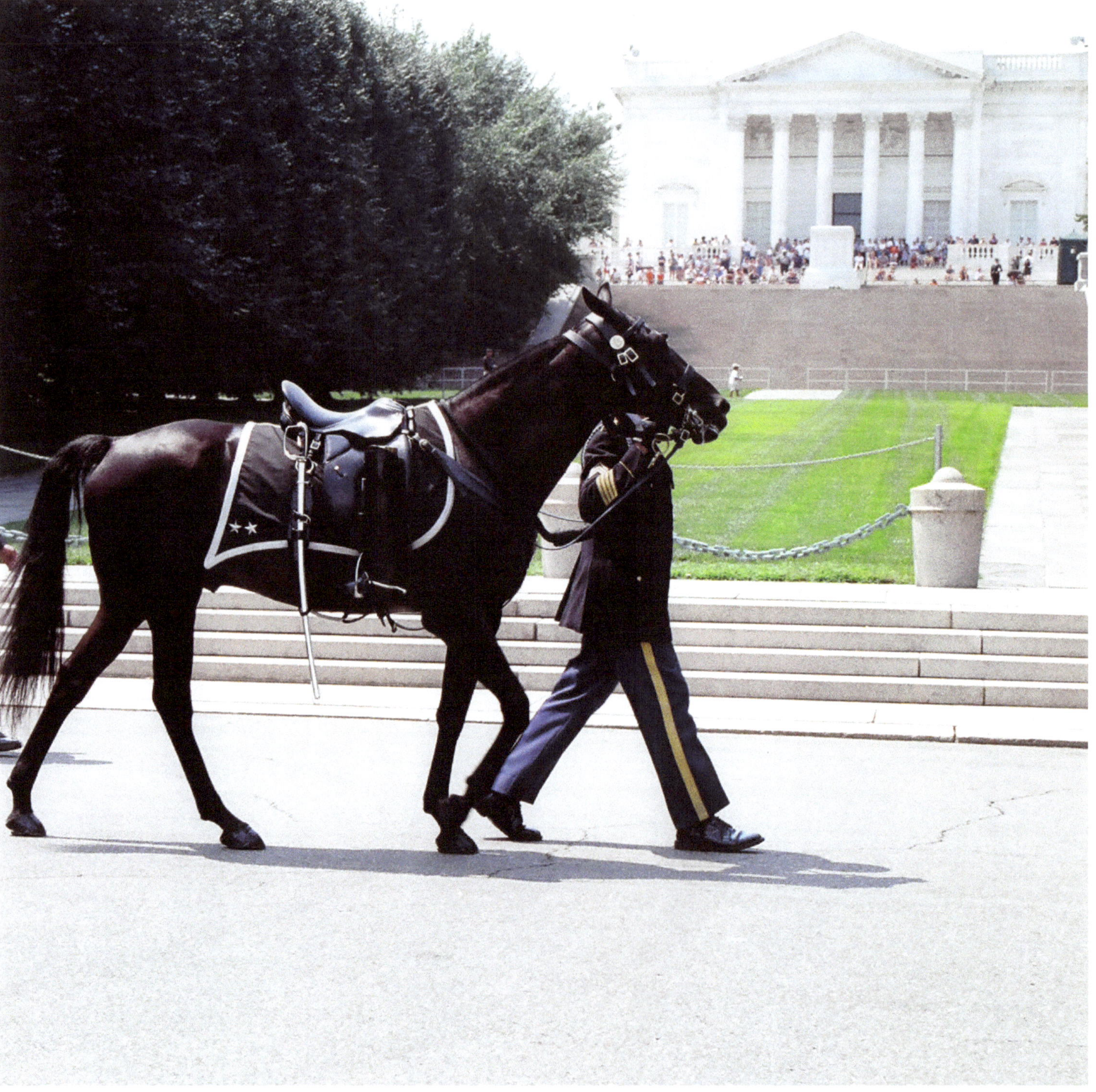

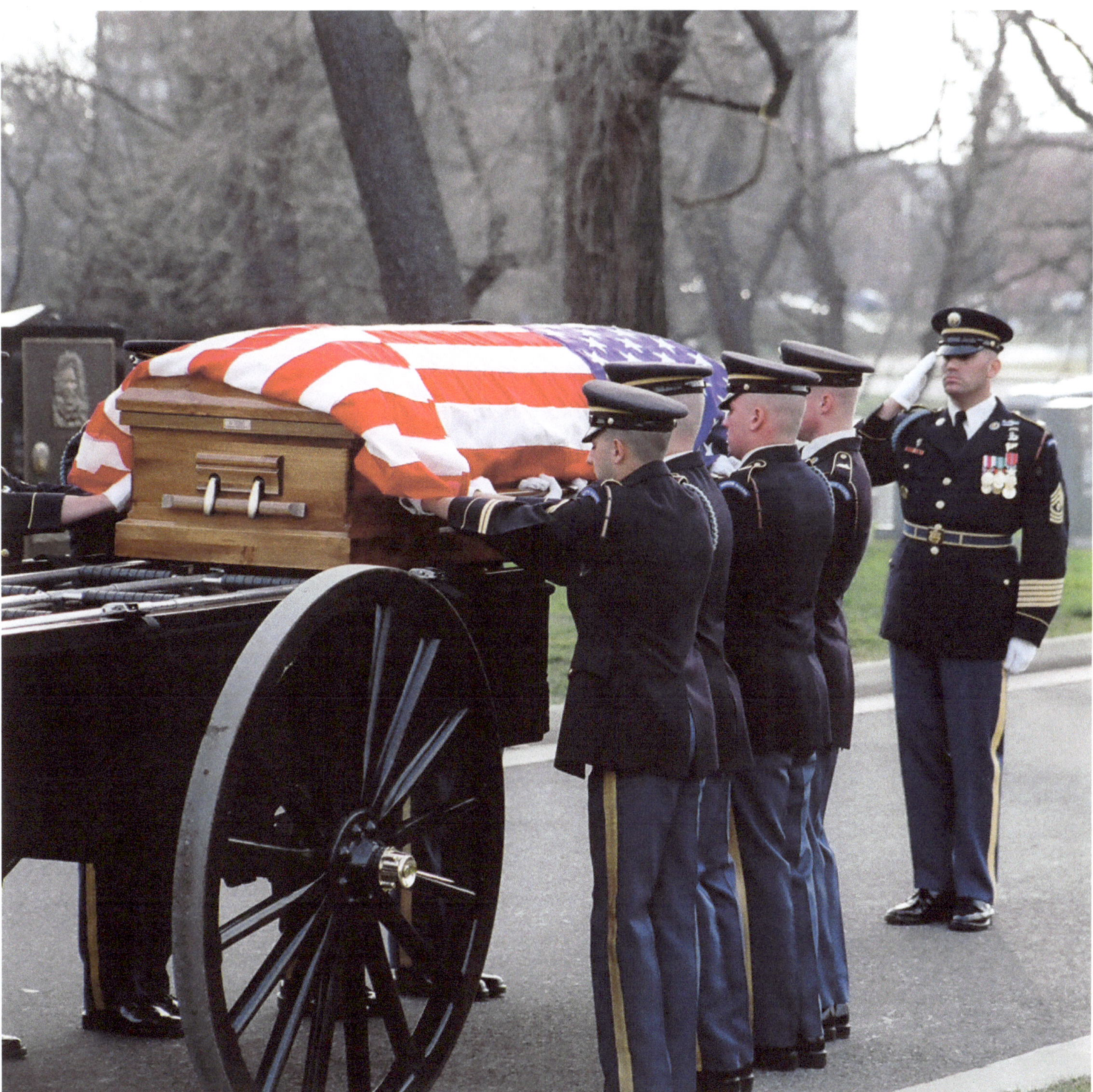

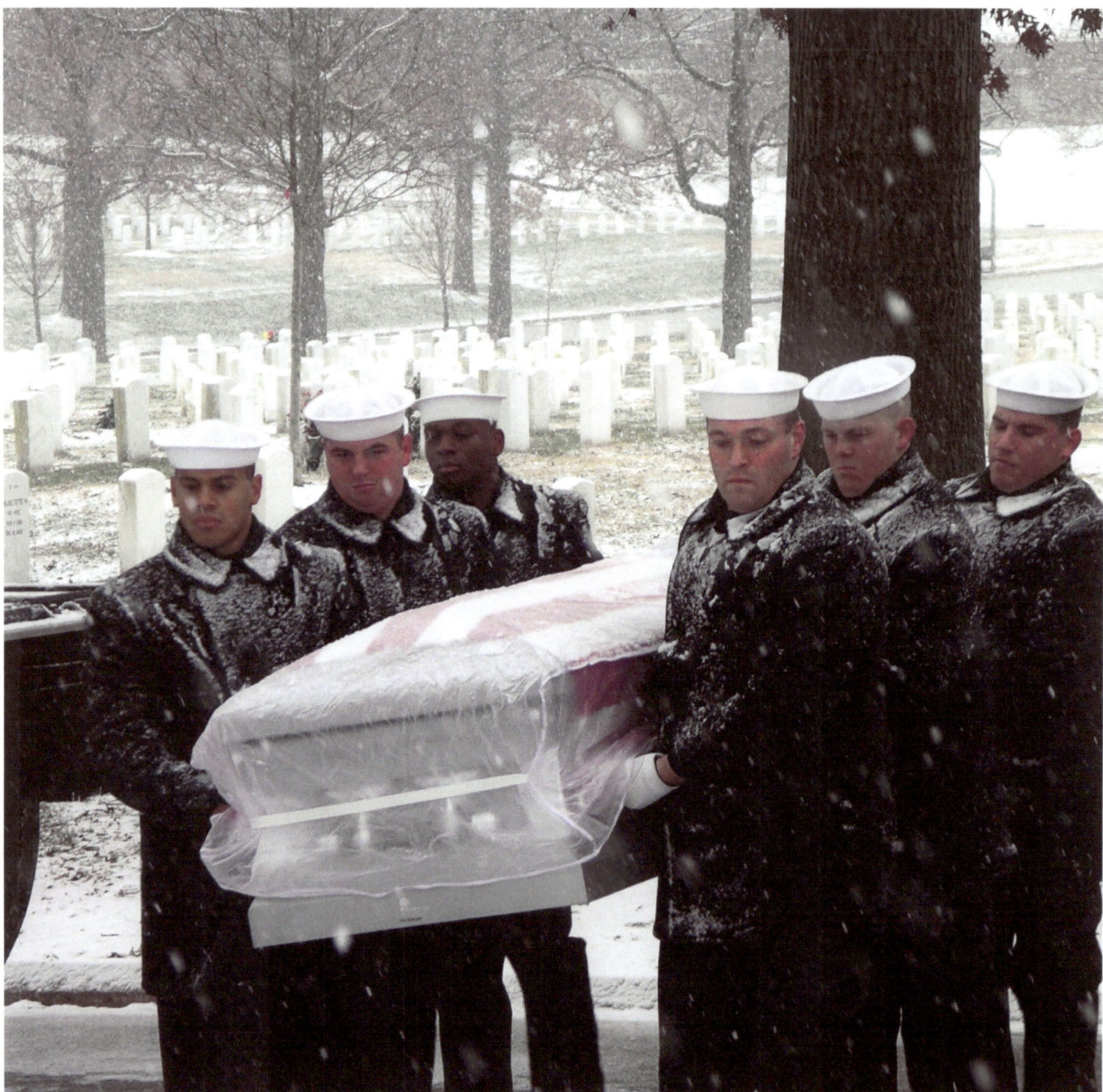

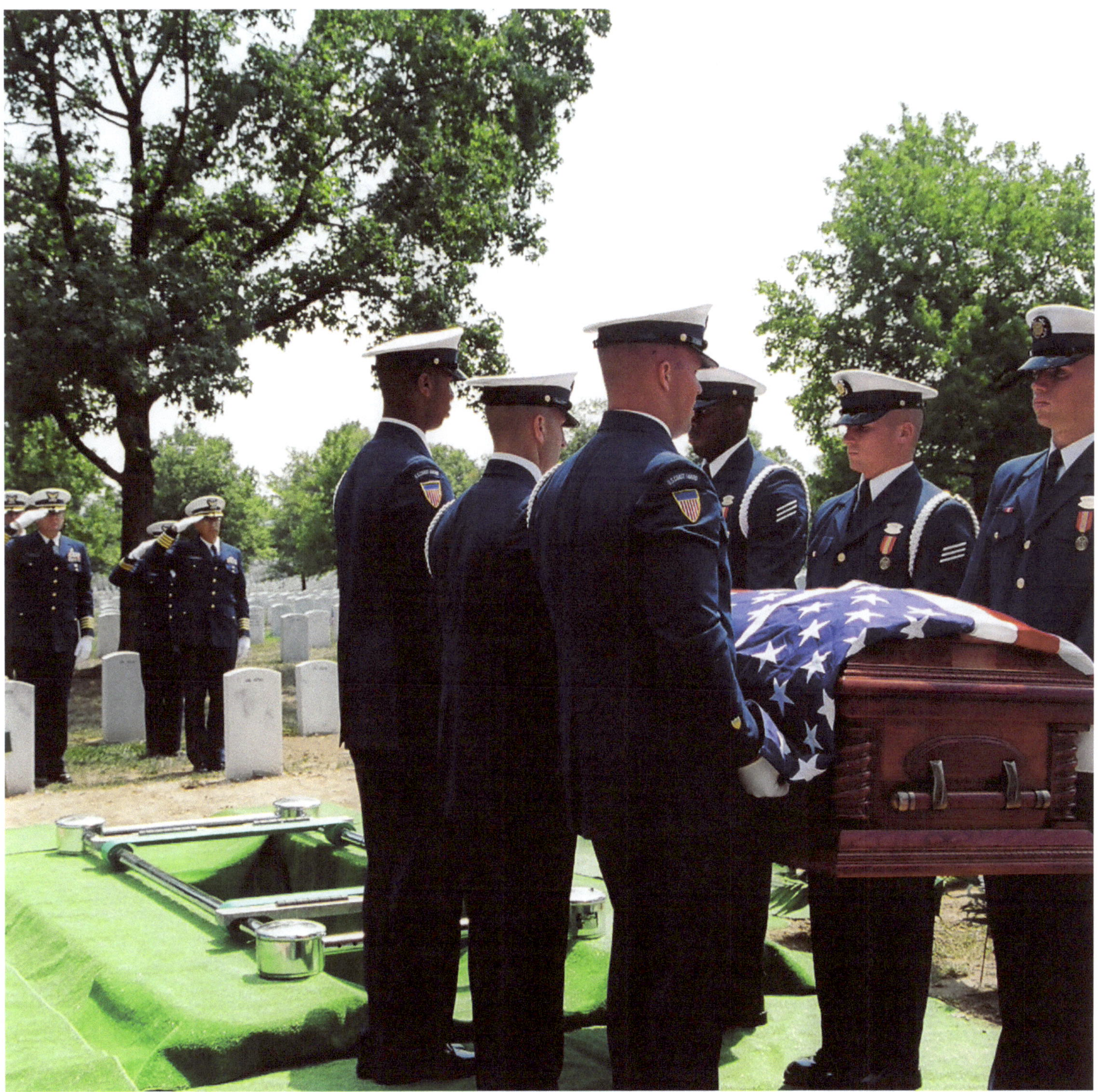

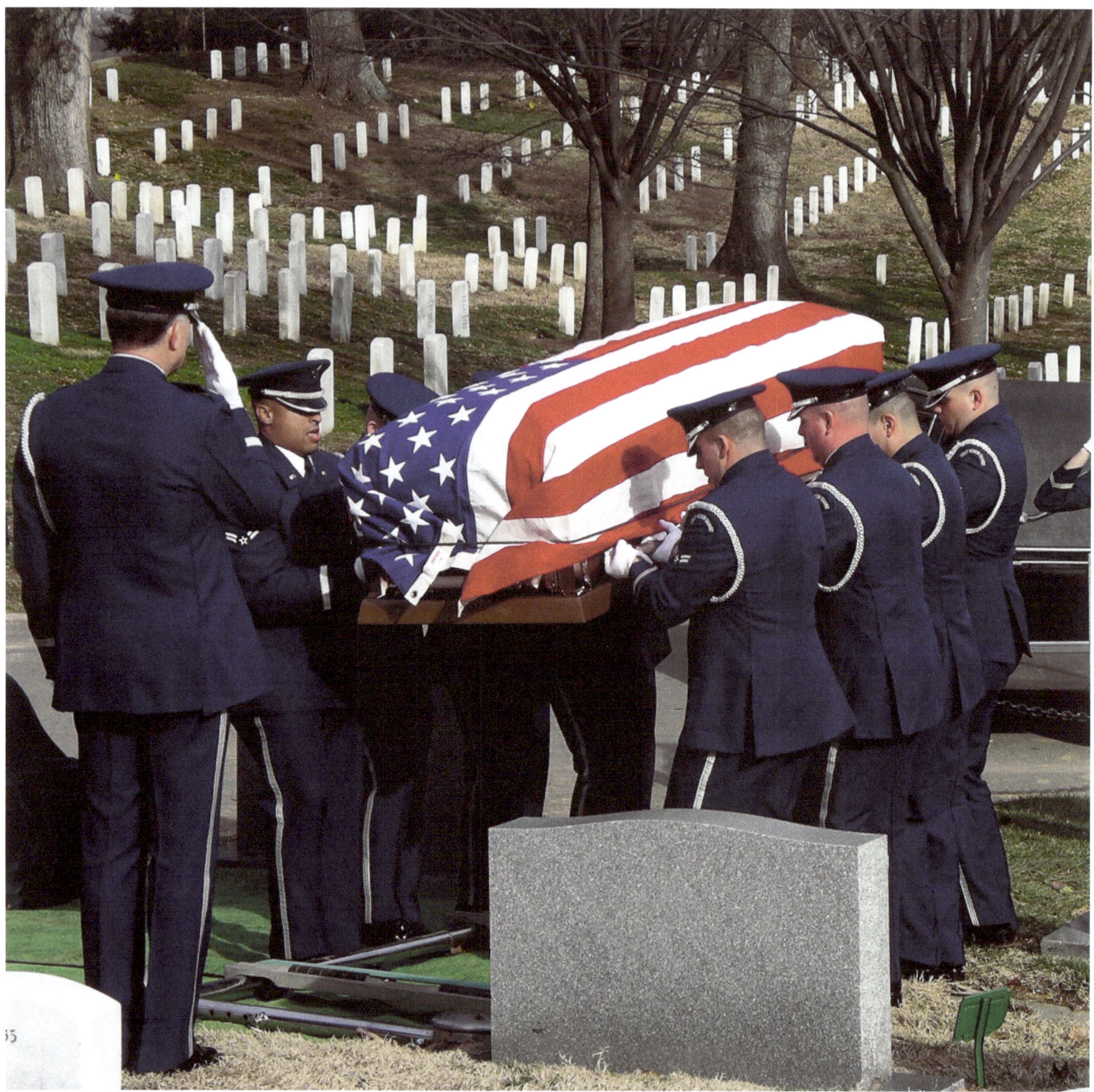

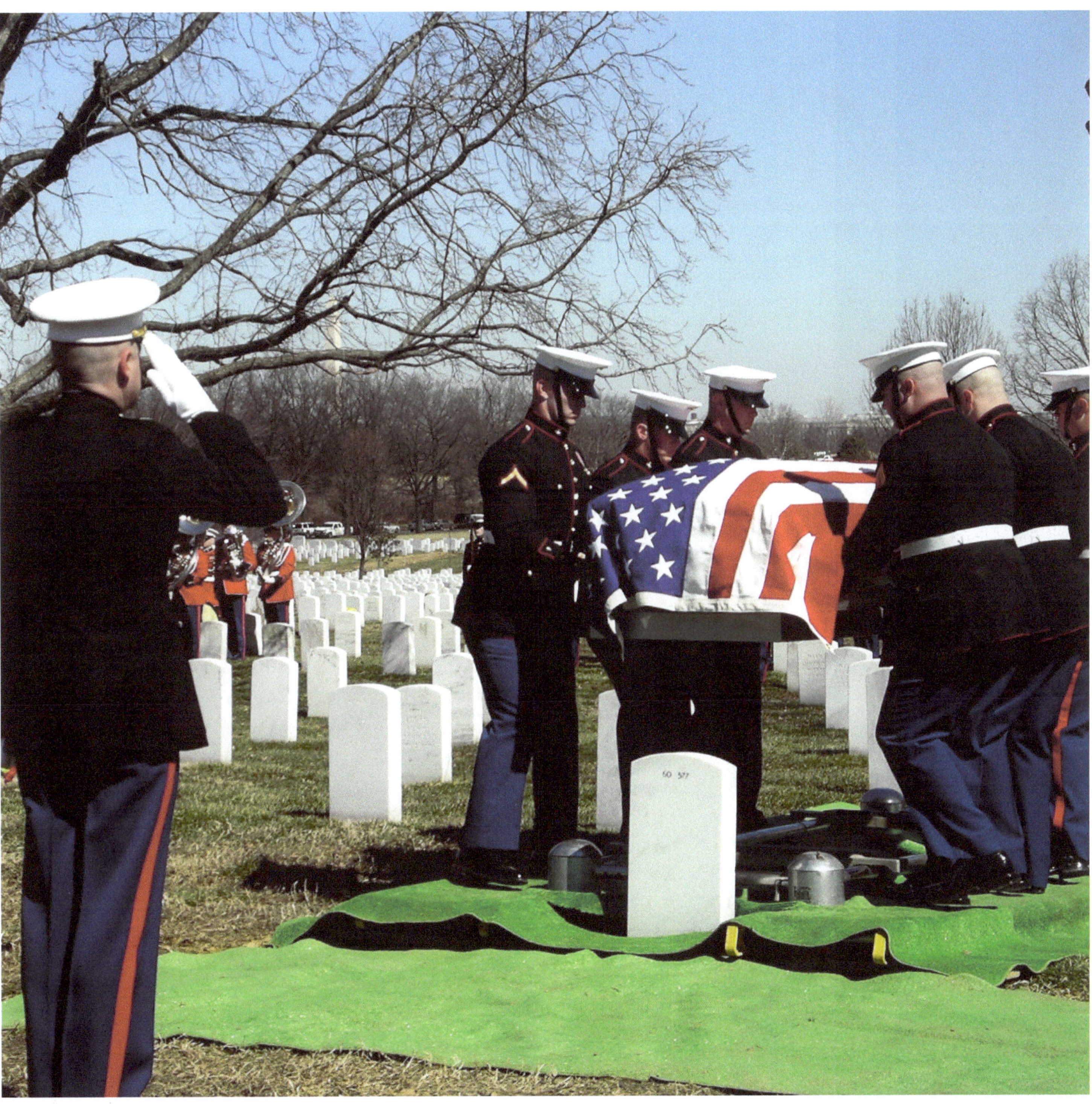

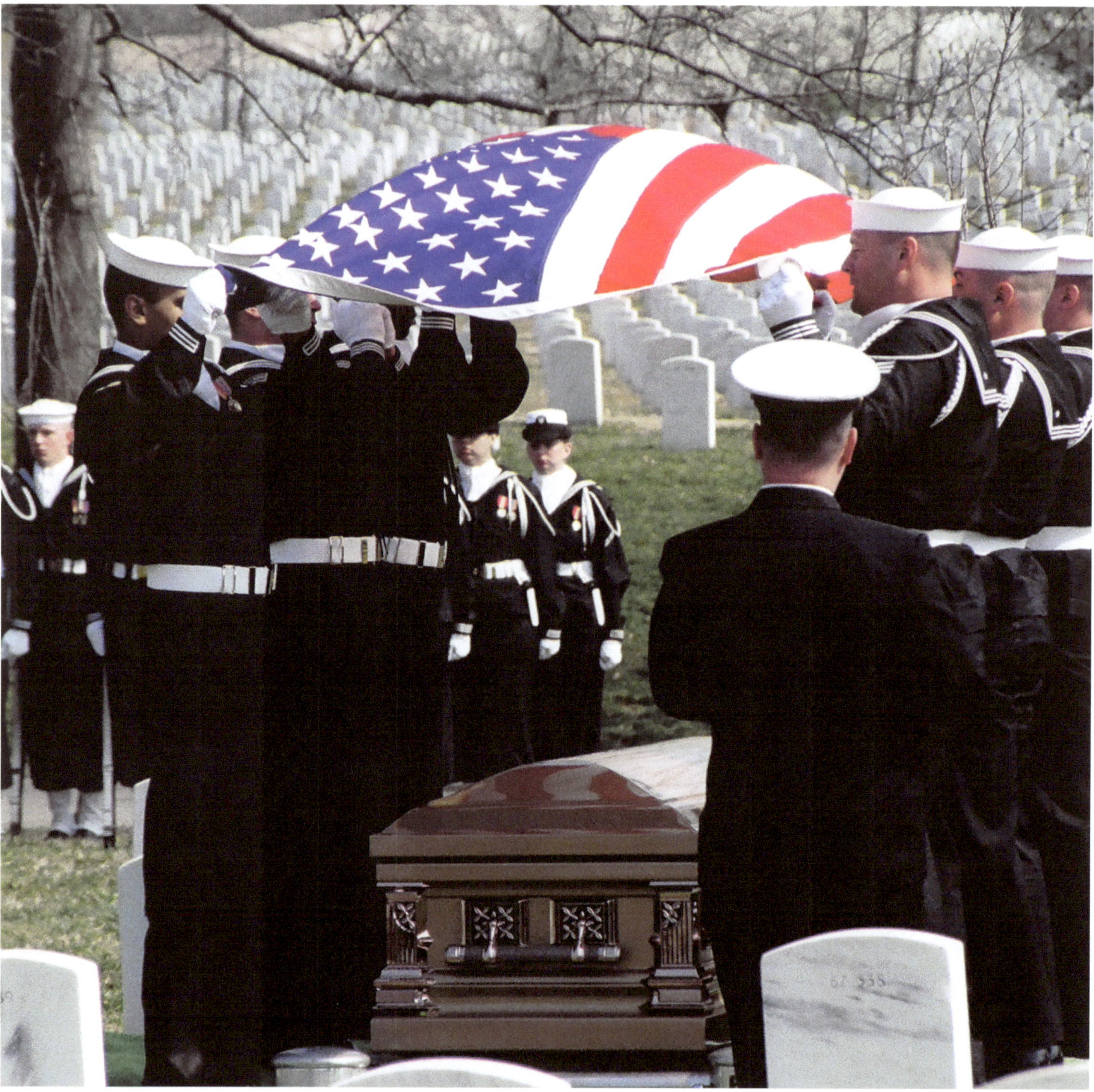

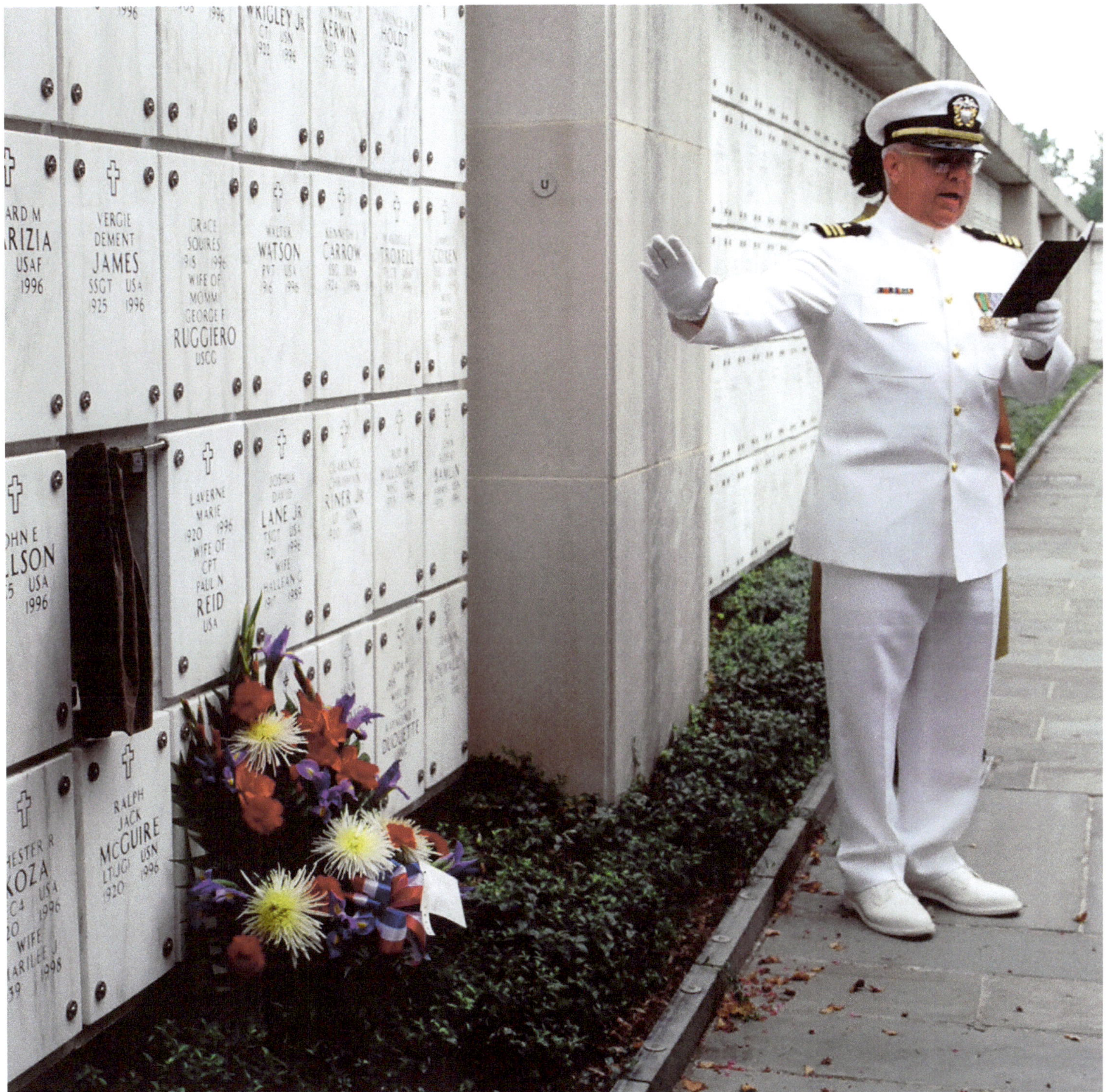

WRIGLEY Jr
KERWIN
HOLDT
VERGIE
DEMENT
JAMES
SSGT USA
1925 1996
GRACE
SQUIRES
WIFE OF
GEORGE F
RUGGIERO
USCG
WATSON
CARROW
ARIZIA
USAF
1996
LAVERNE
MARIE
1920 1996
WIFE OF
CPT
PAUL N
REID
USA
LANE Jr
RINER Jr
RALPH
JACK
McGUIRE
LTJG USN
1920 1996
KOZA

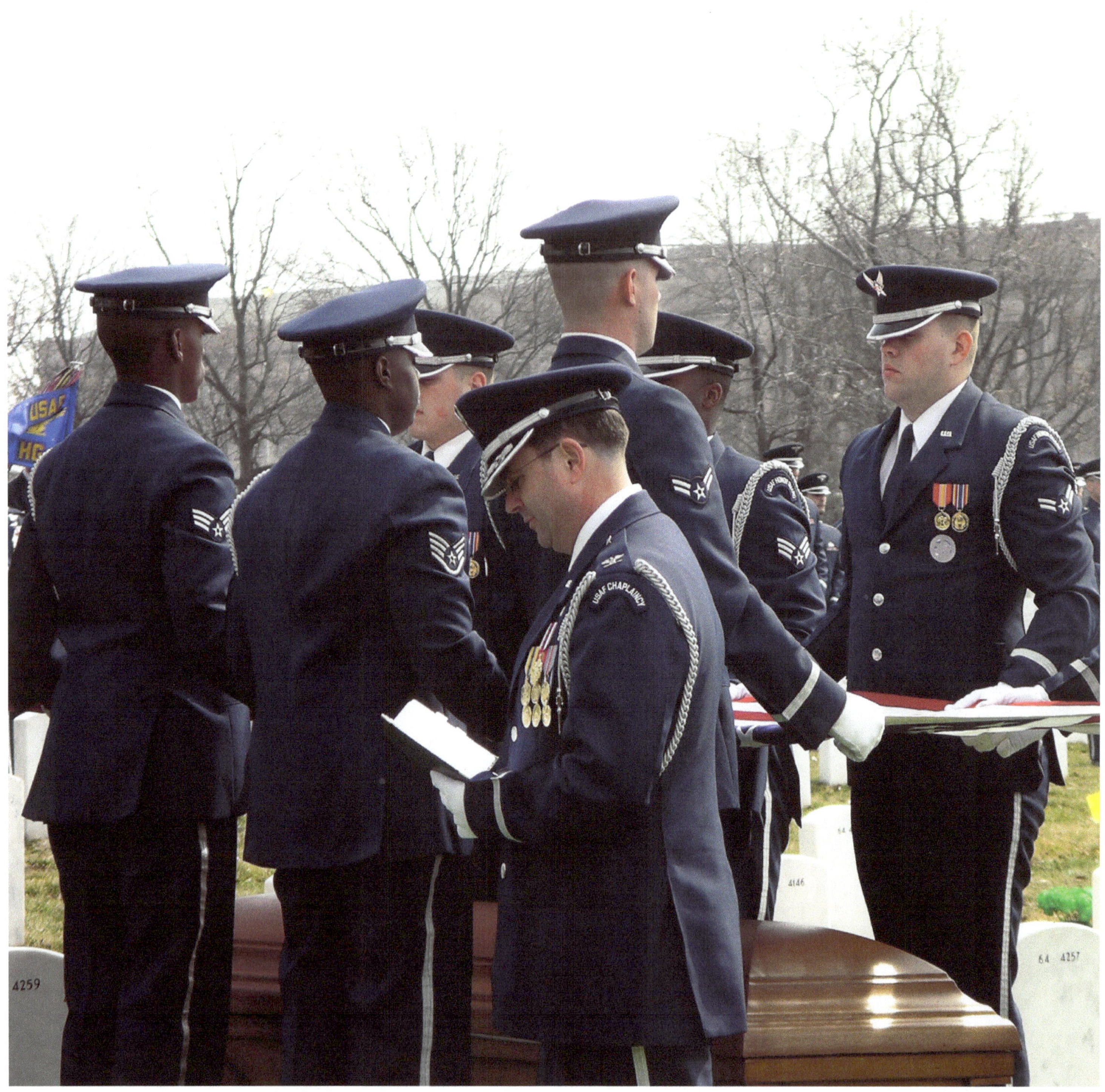
USAF
USAF CHAPLAINCY
4146
4259
64 4257

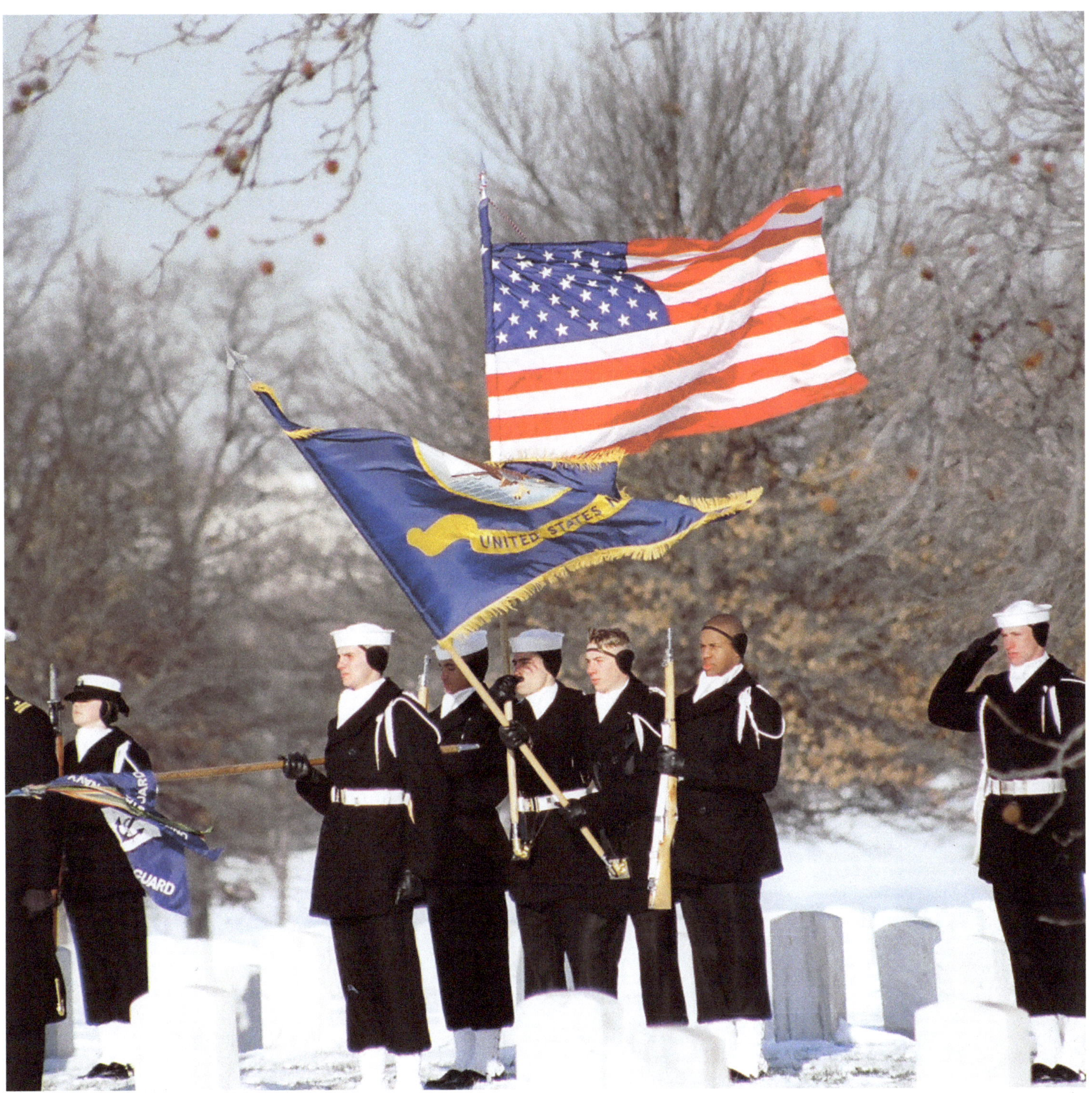
UNITED STATES
GUARD

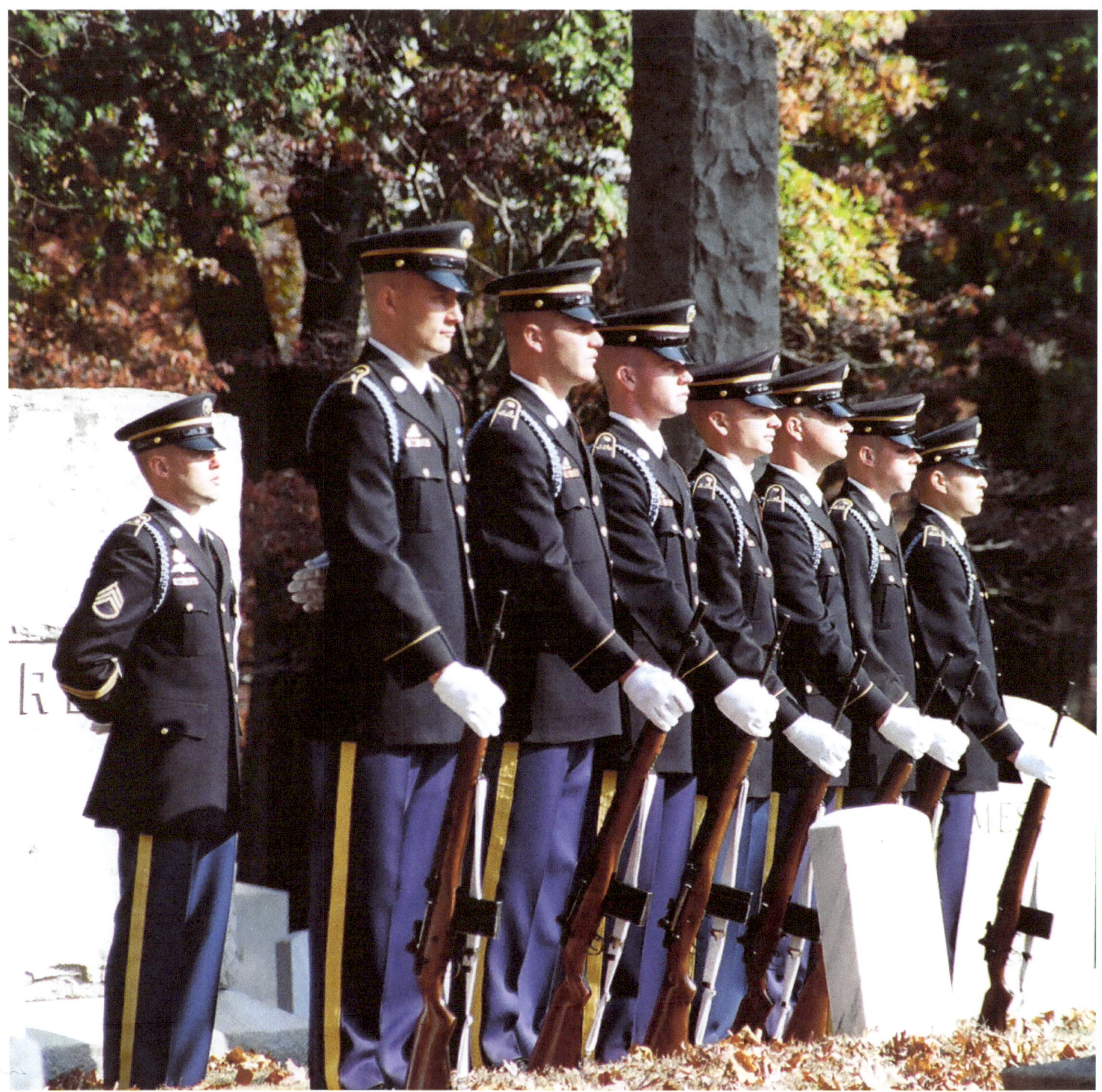

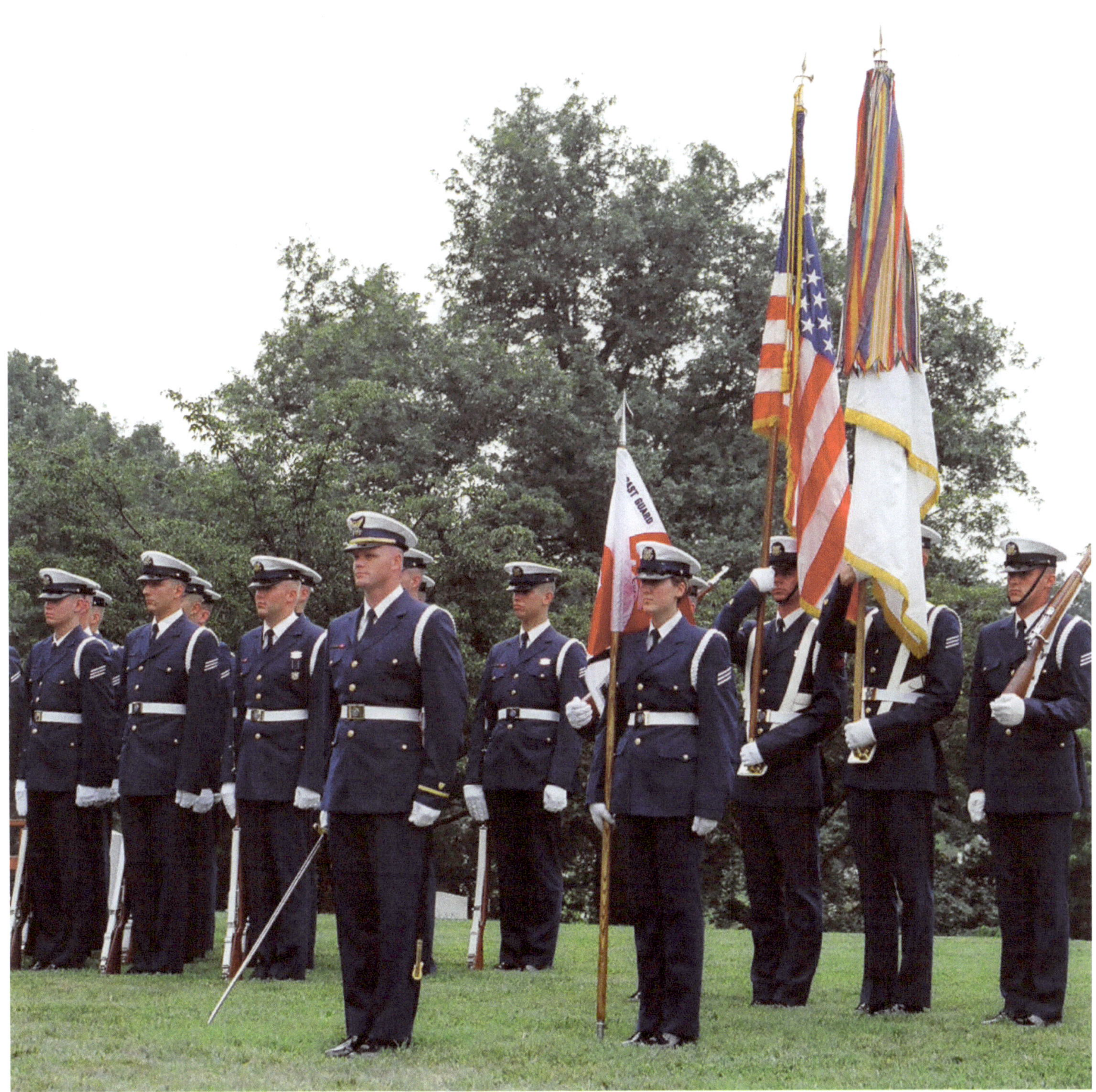

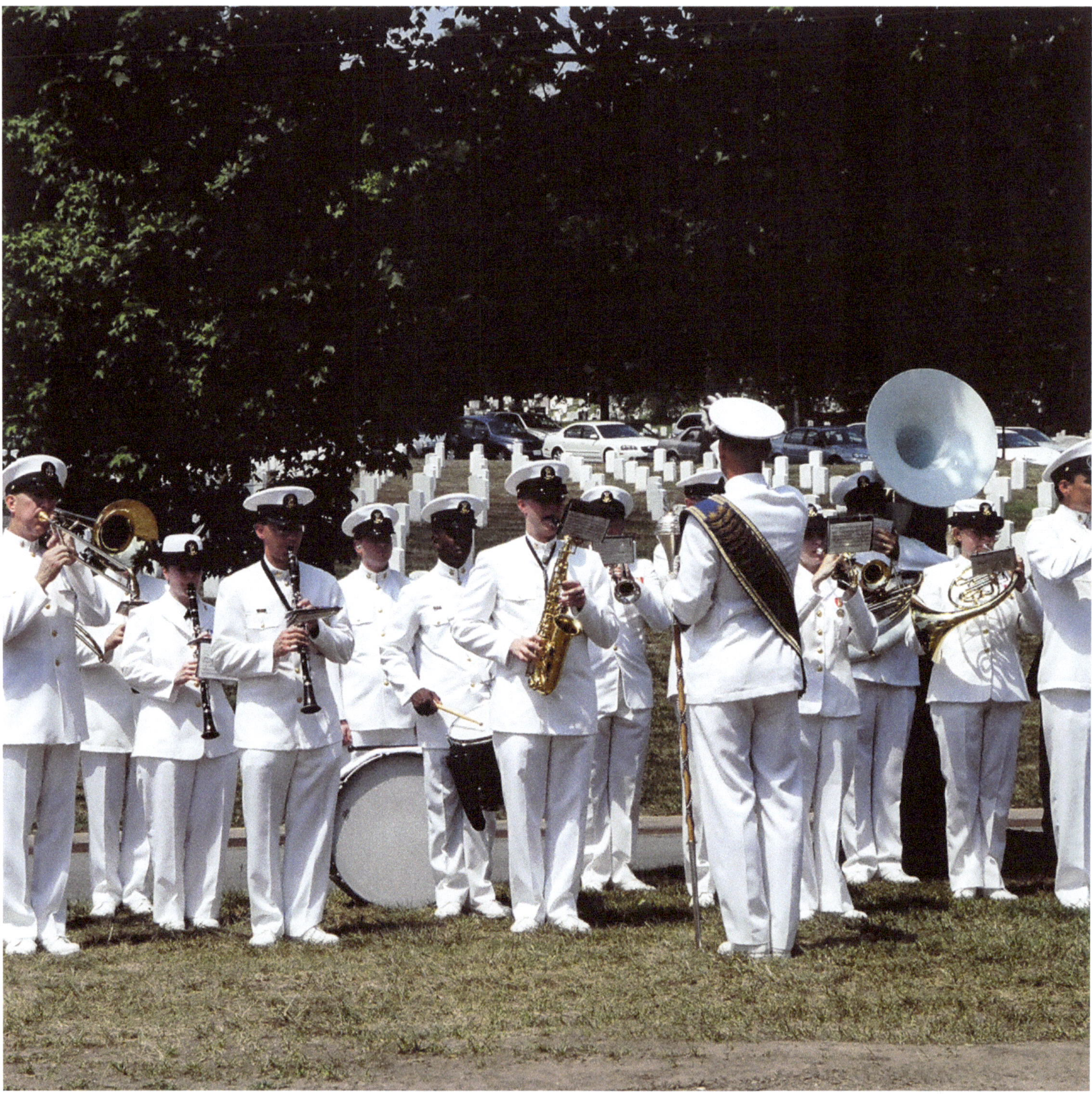

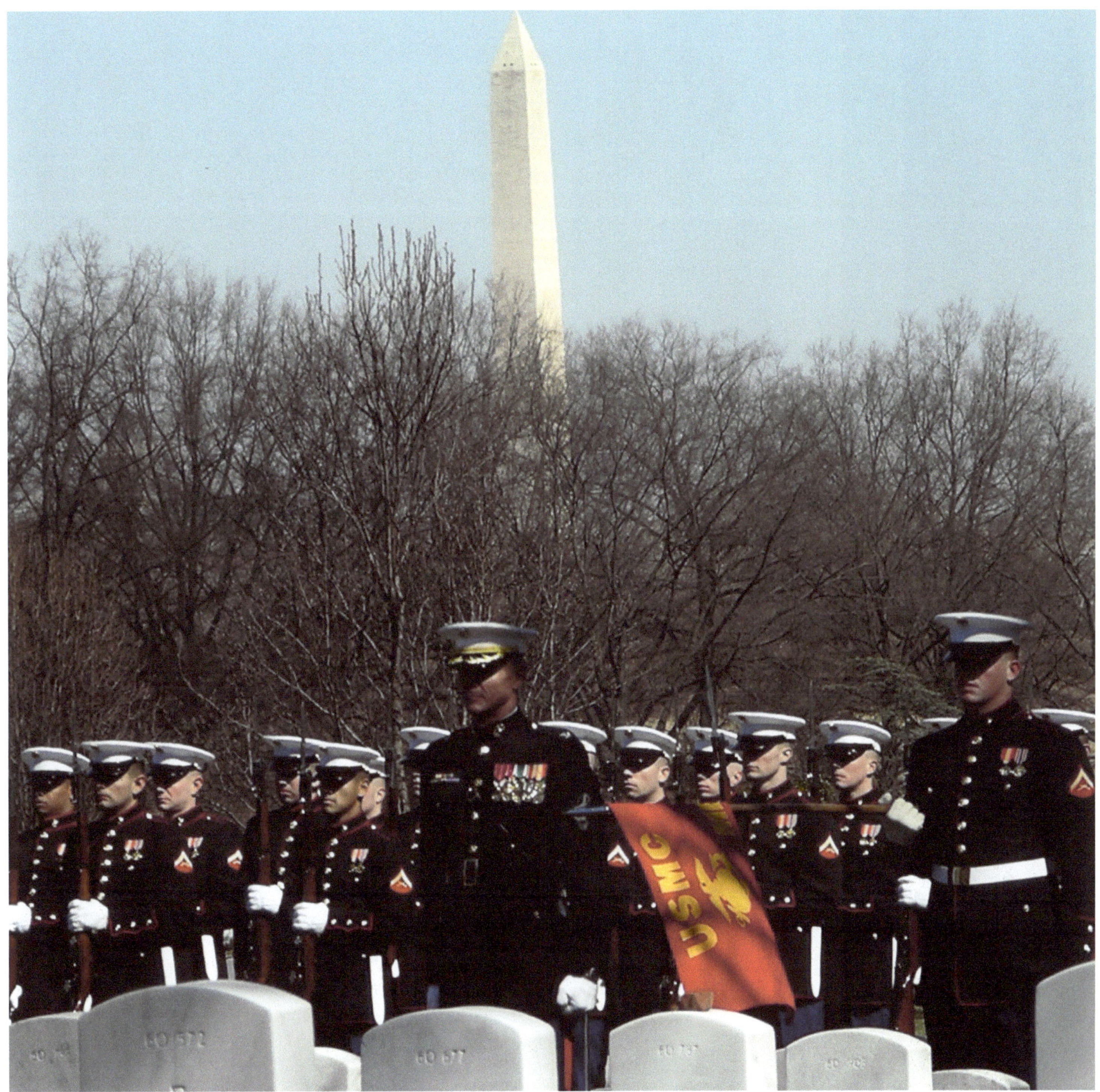
USMC

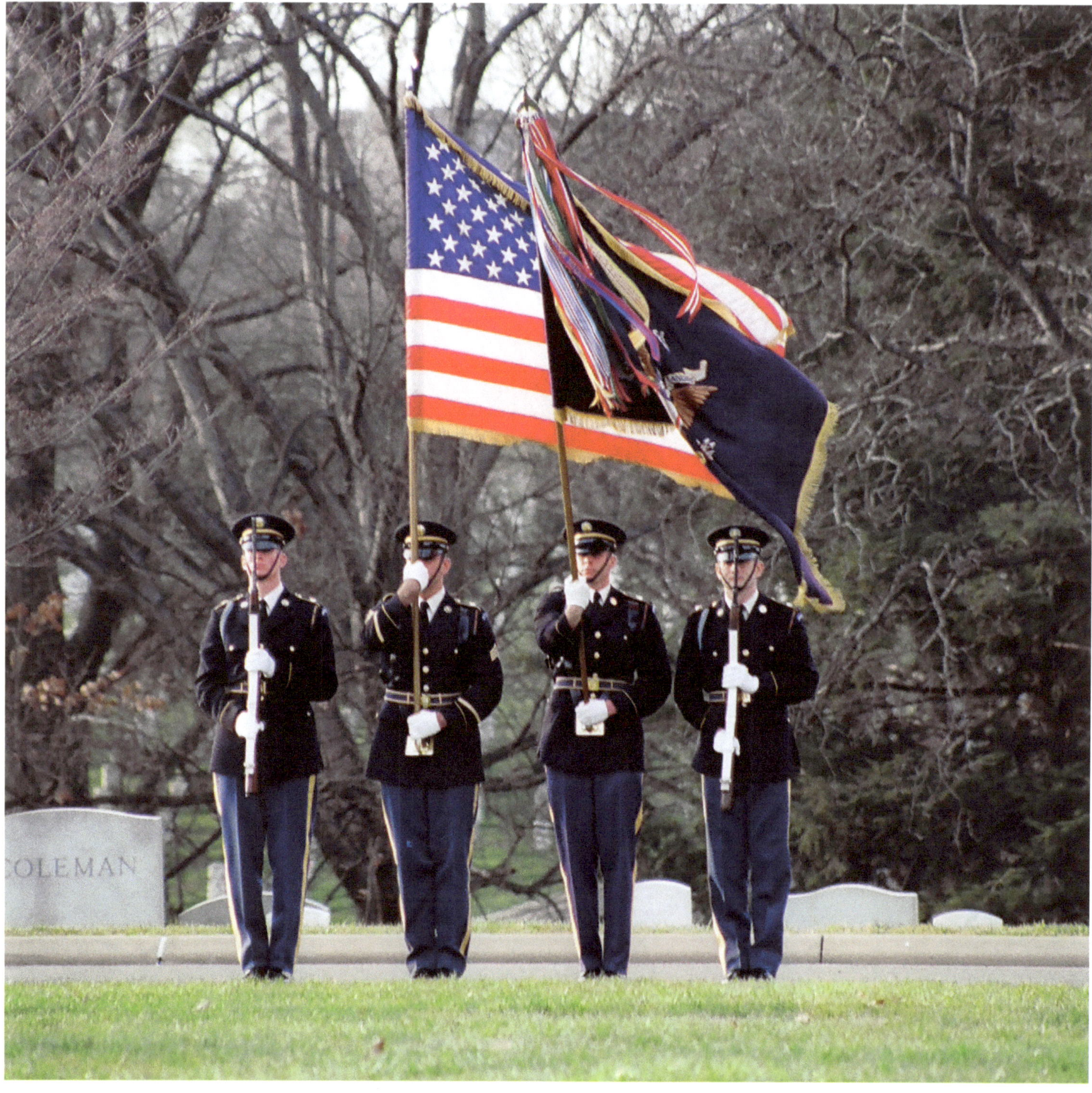
COLEMAN

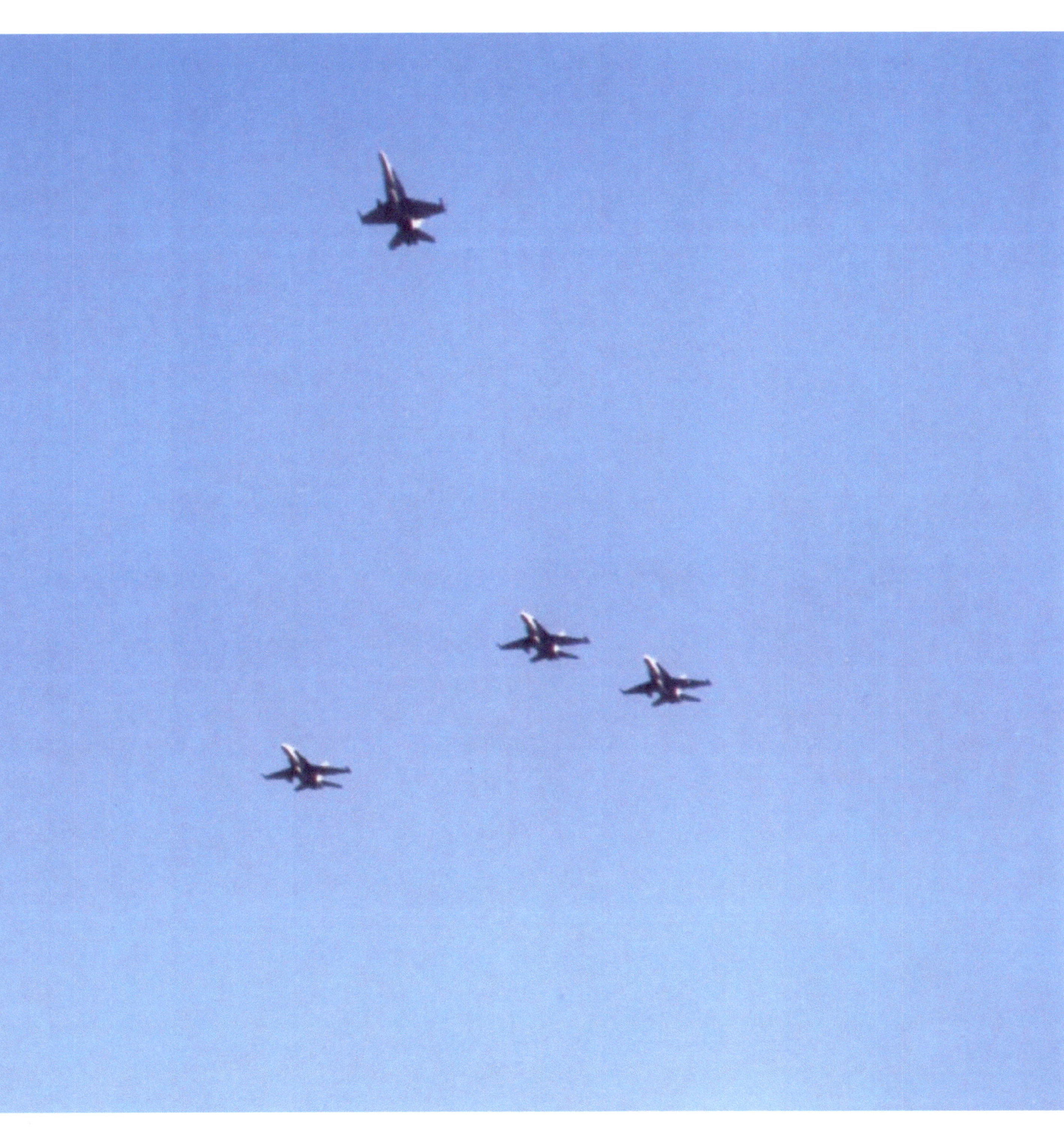

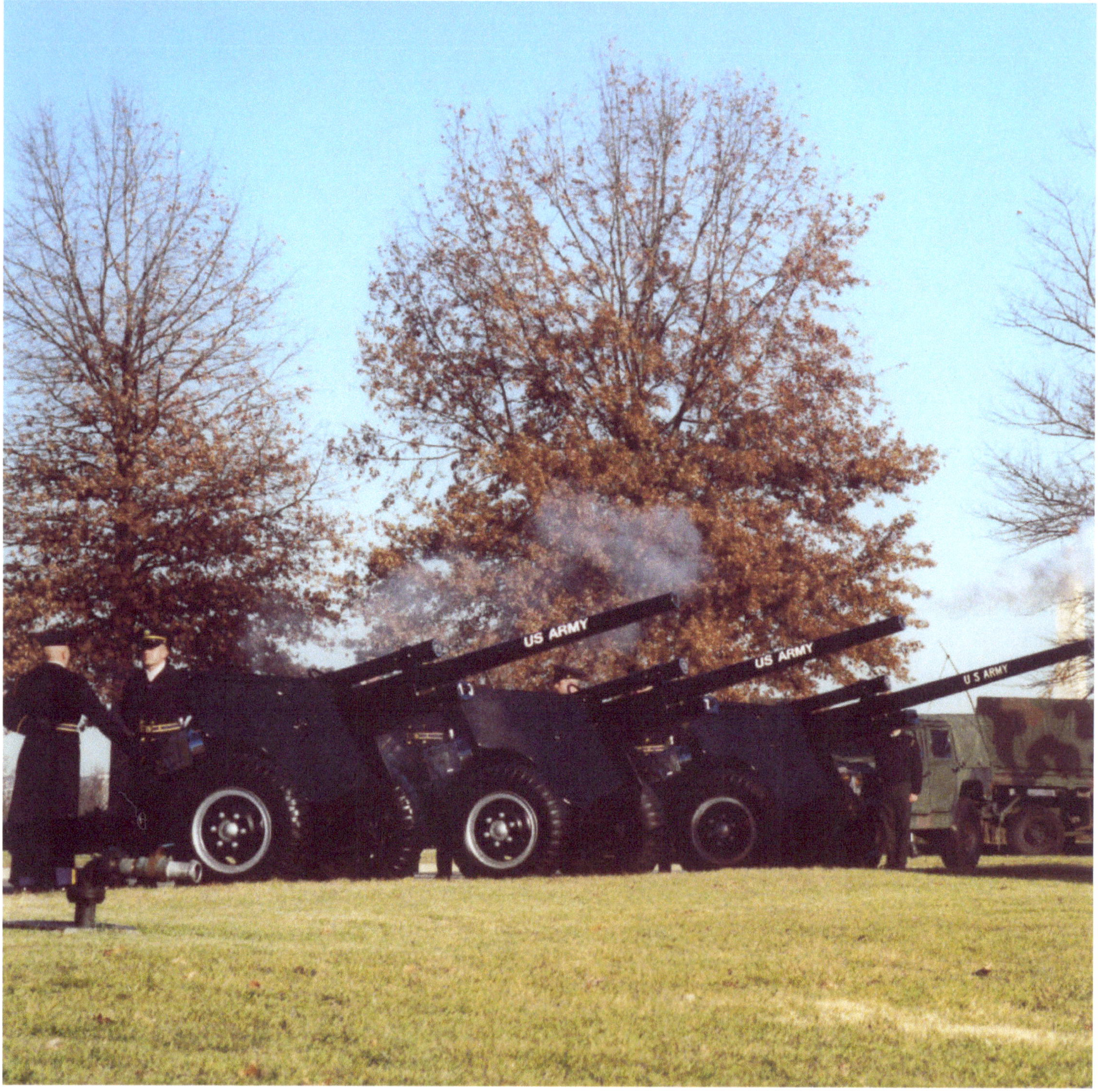
US ARMY
US ARMY
U.S. ARMY

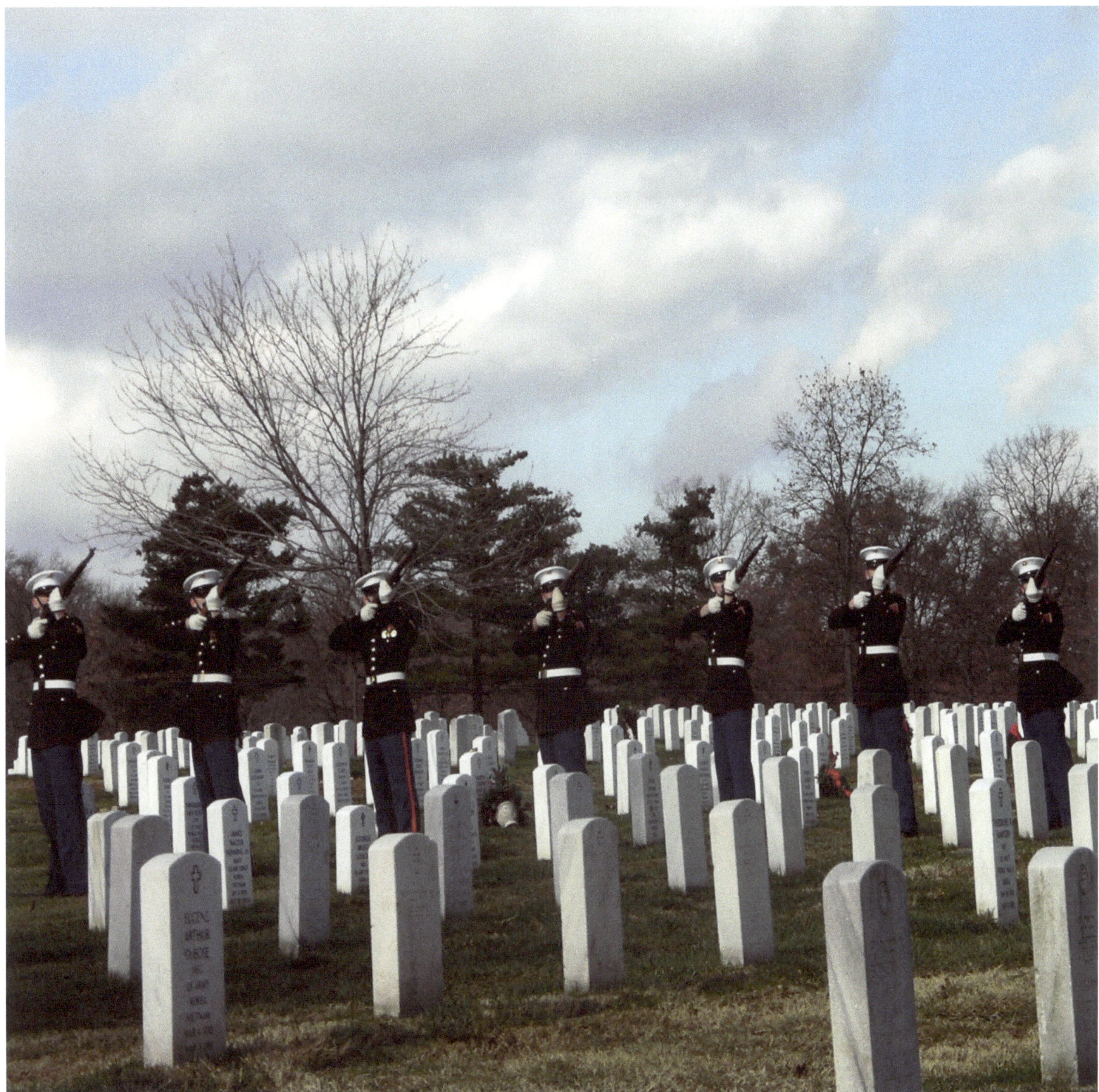

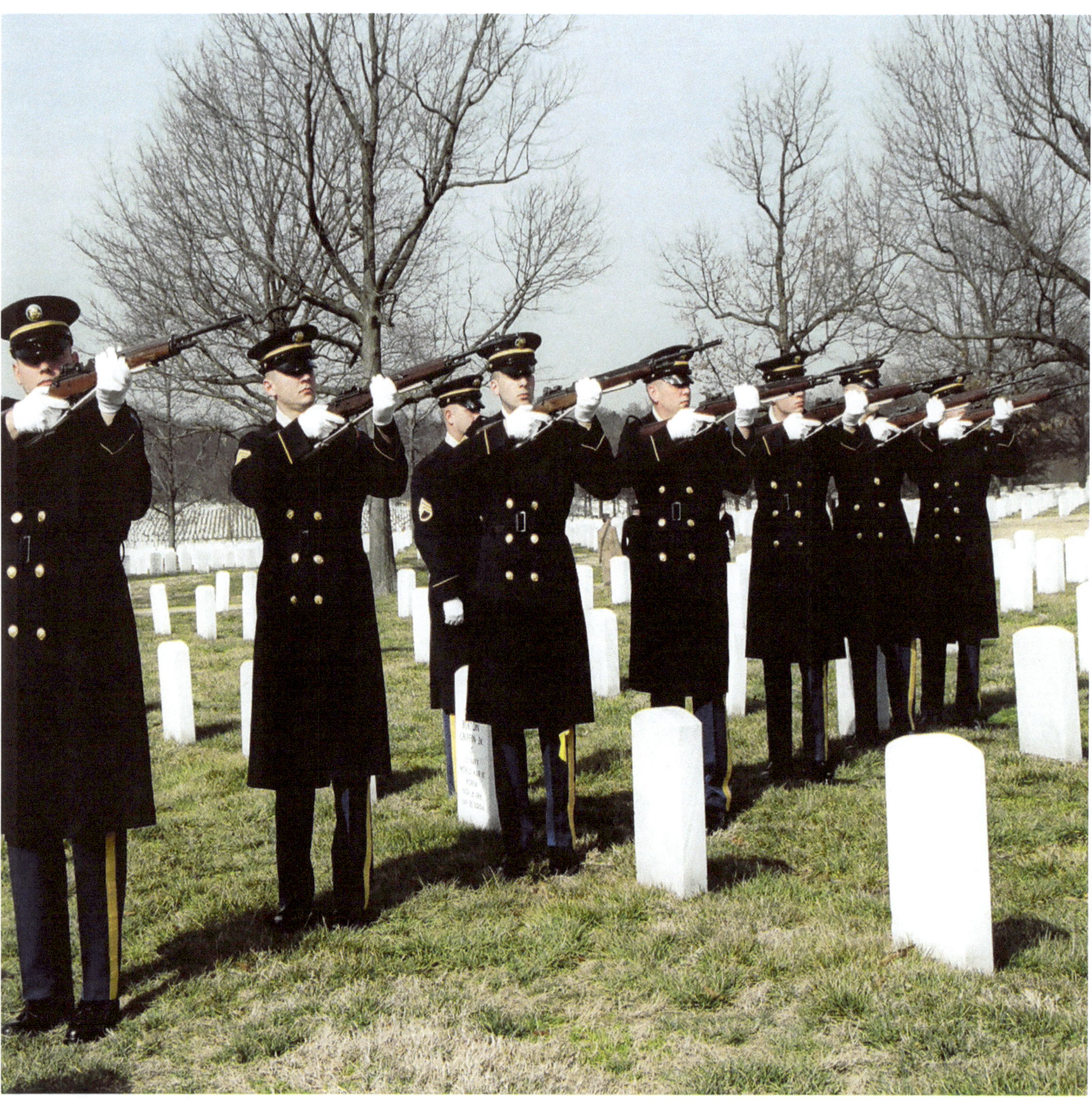

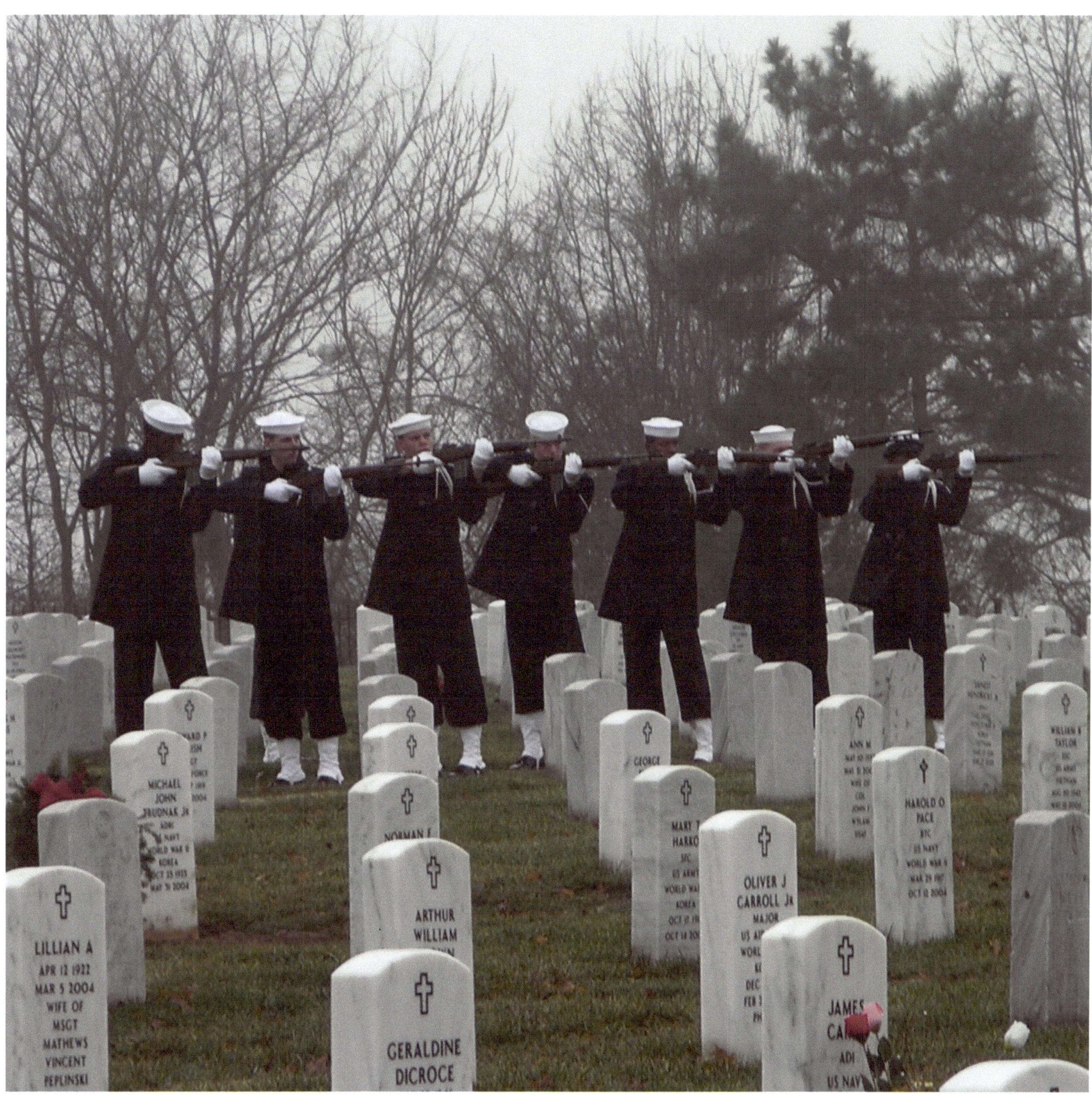
LILLIAN A
APR 12 1922
MAR 5 2004
WIFE OF
MSGT
MATHEWS
VINCENT
PEPLINSKI
GERALDINE
DICROCE
ARTHUR
WILLIAM
OLIVER J
CARROLL JR
MAJOR
HAROLD O
PACE
MICHAEL
JOHN
JAMES
US NAVY

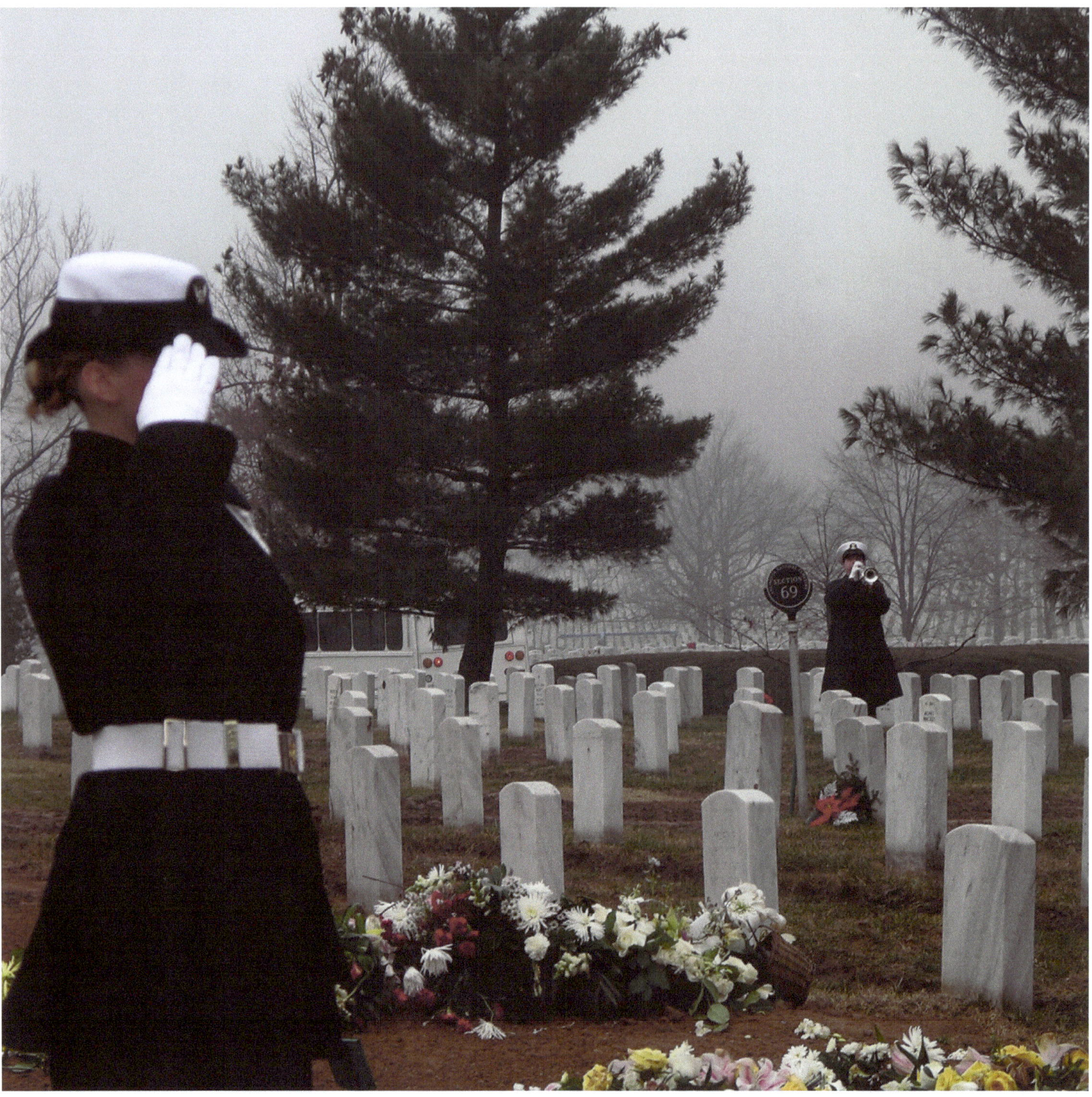
69

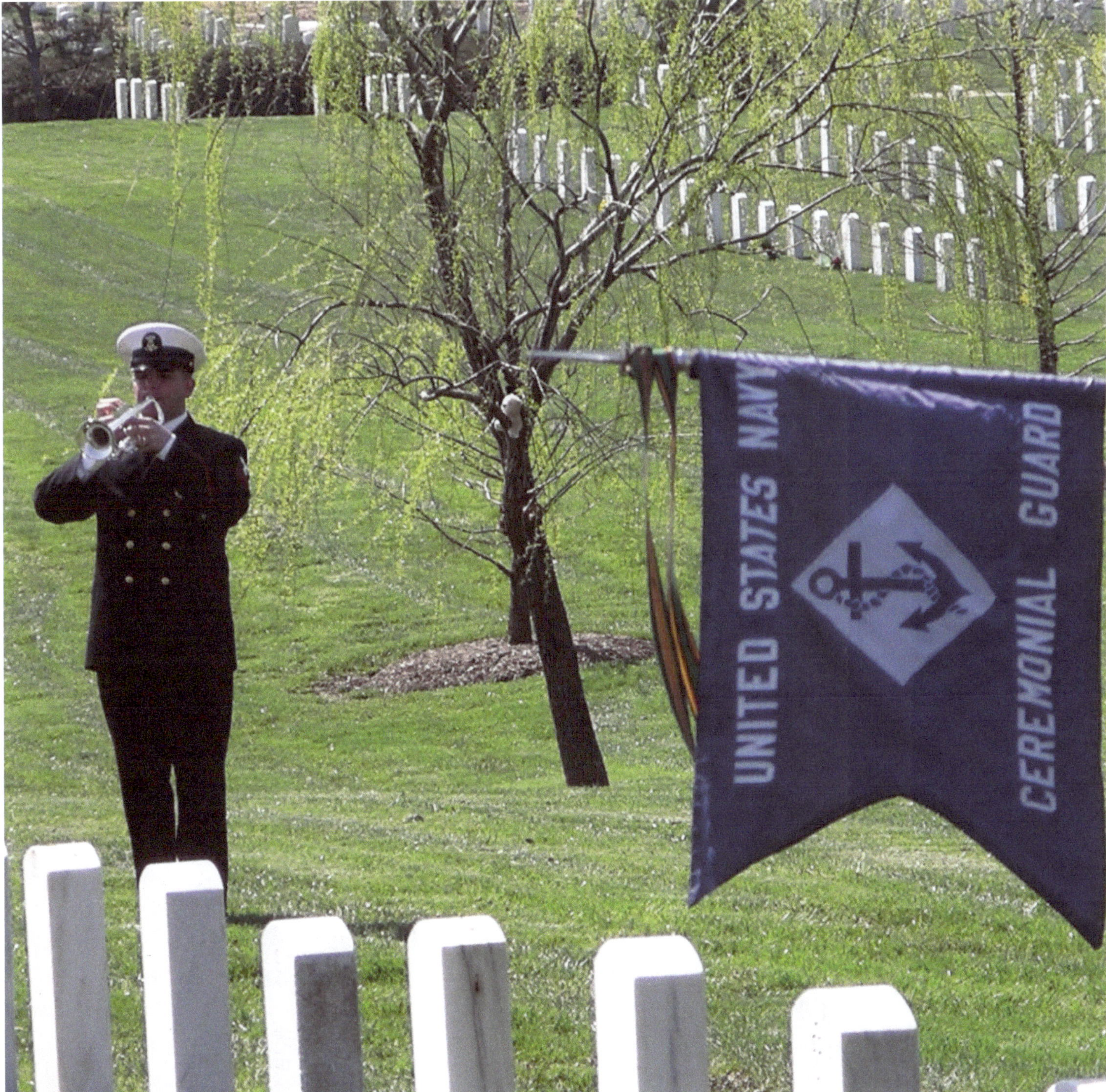
UNITED STATES NAVY
CEREMONIAL GUARD

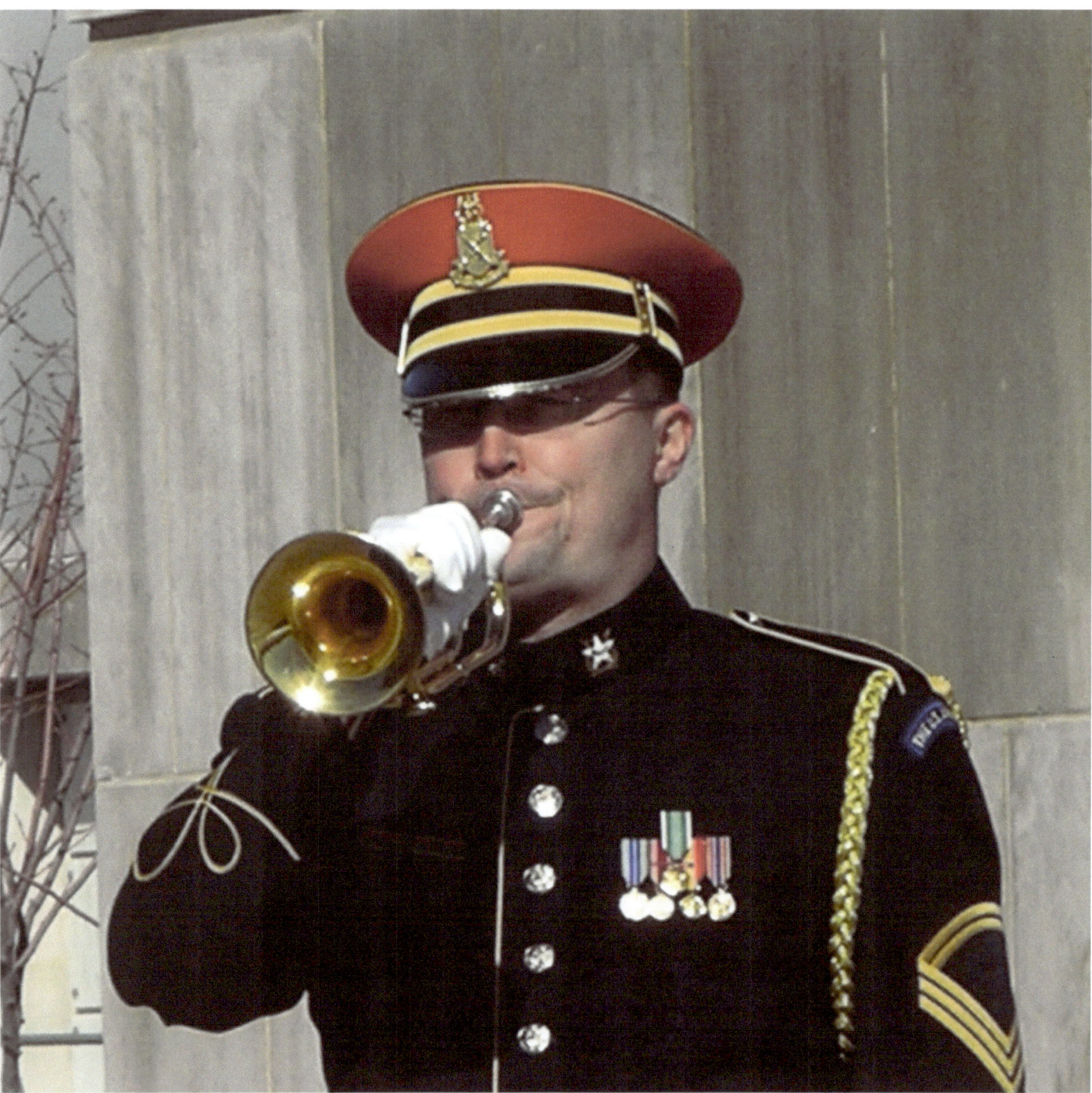

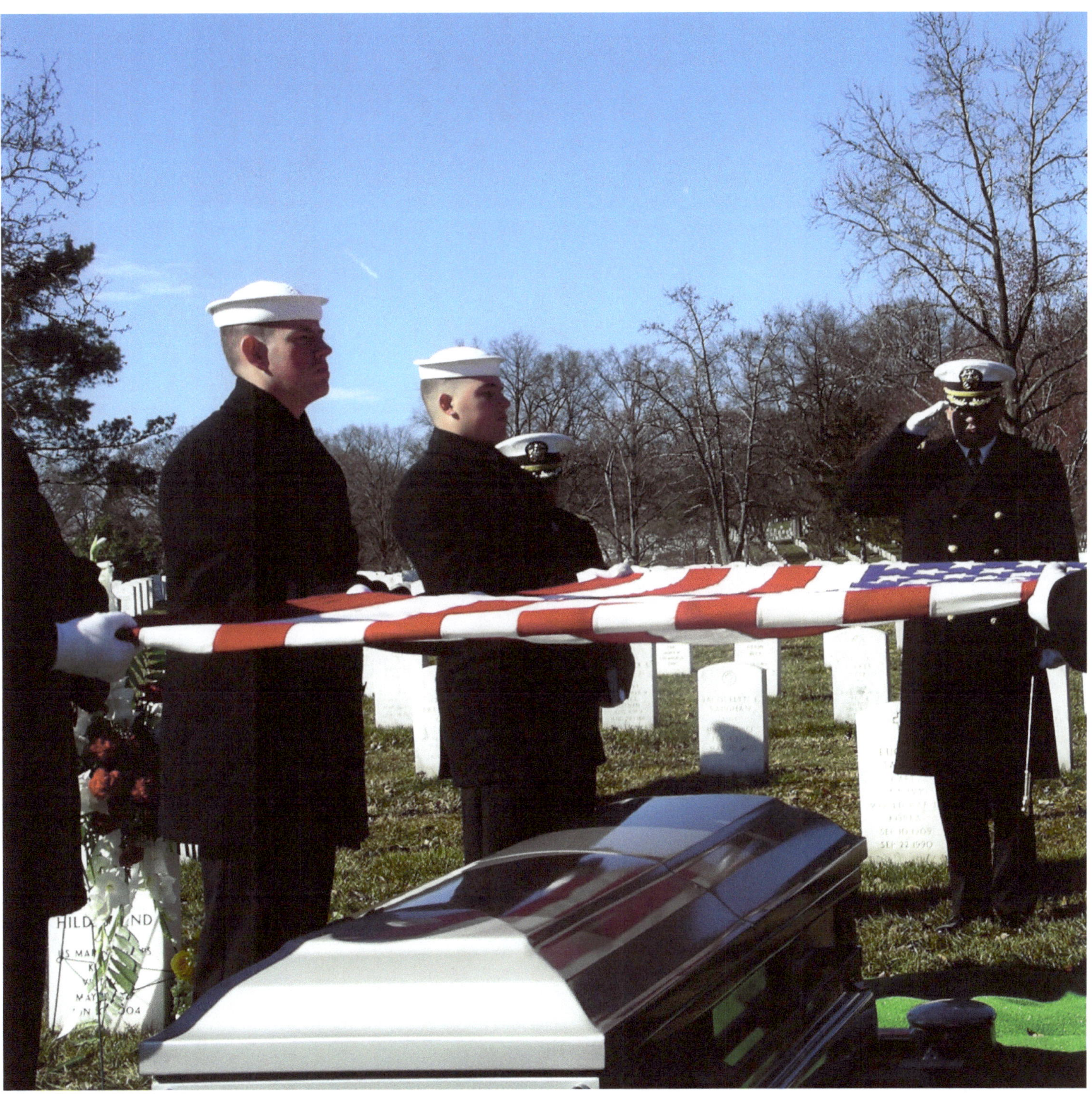

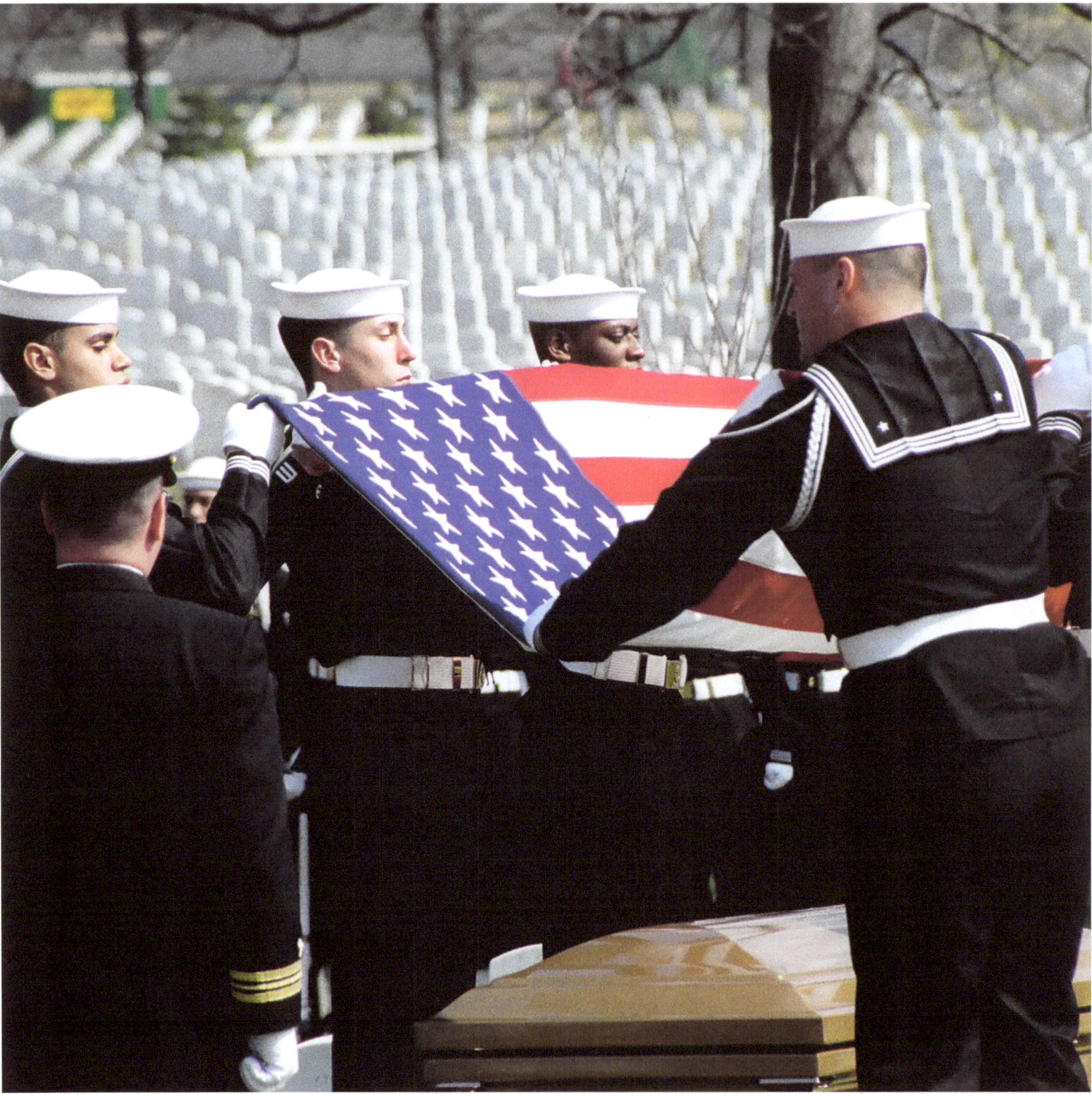

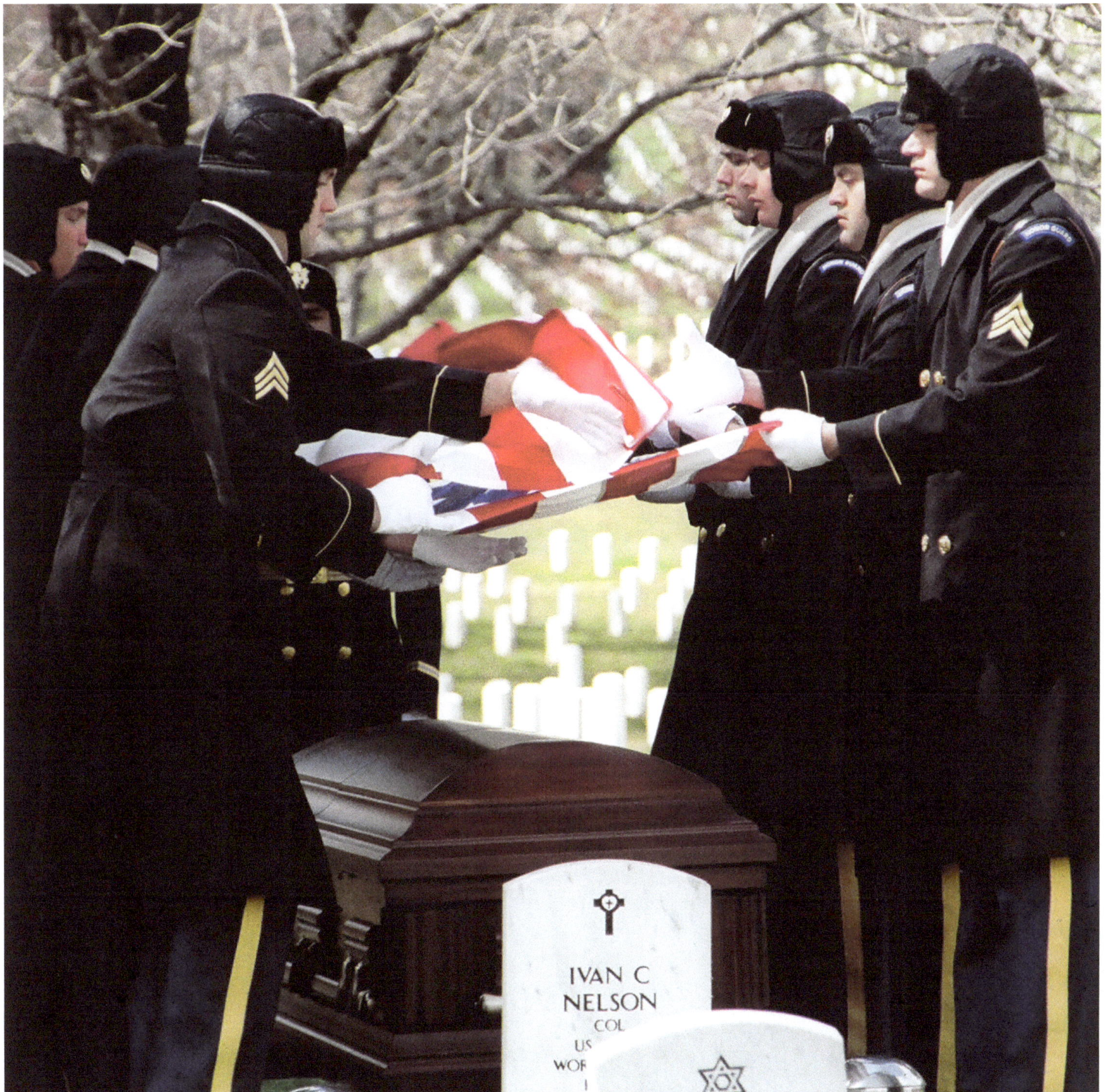
IVAN C
NELSON
COL
US

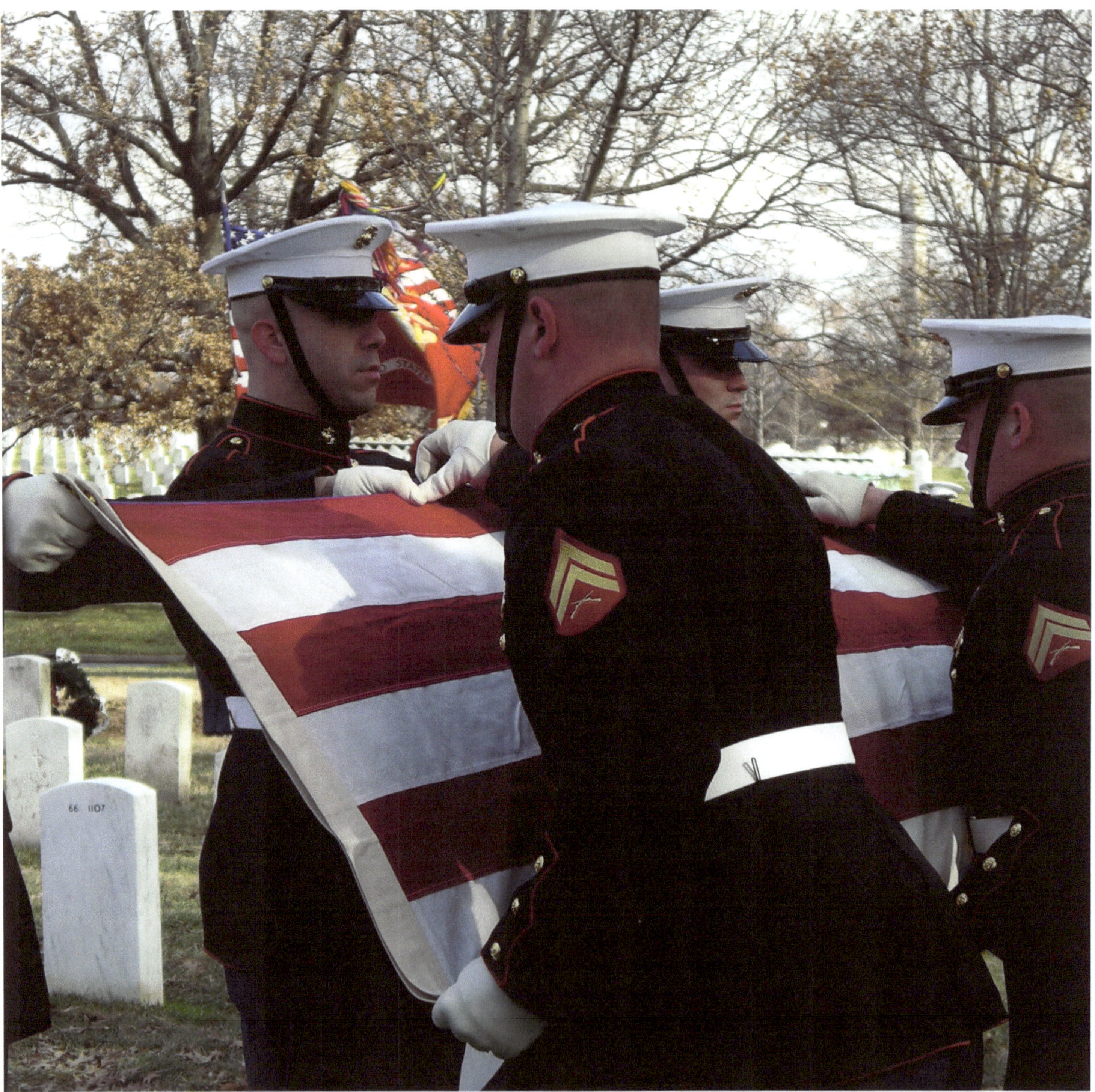
66 1107

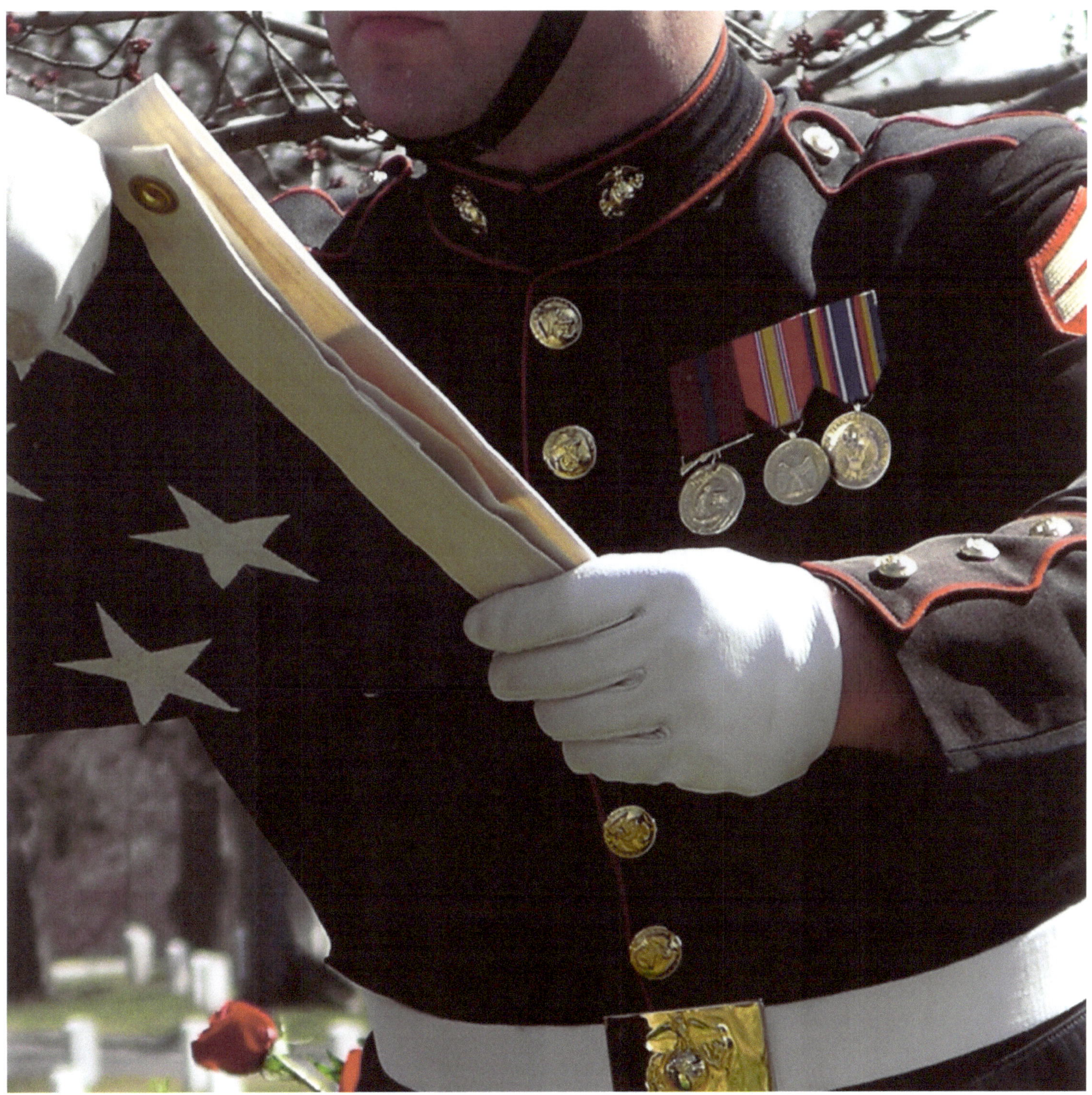

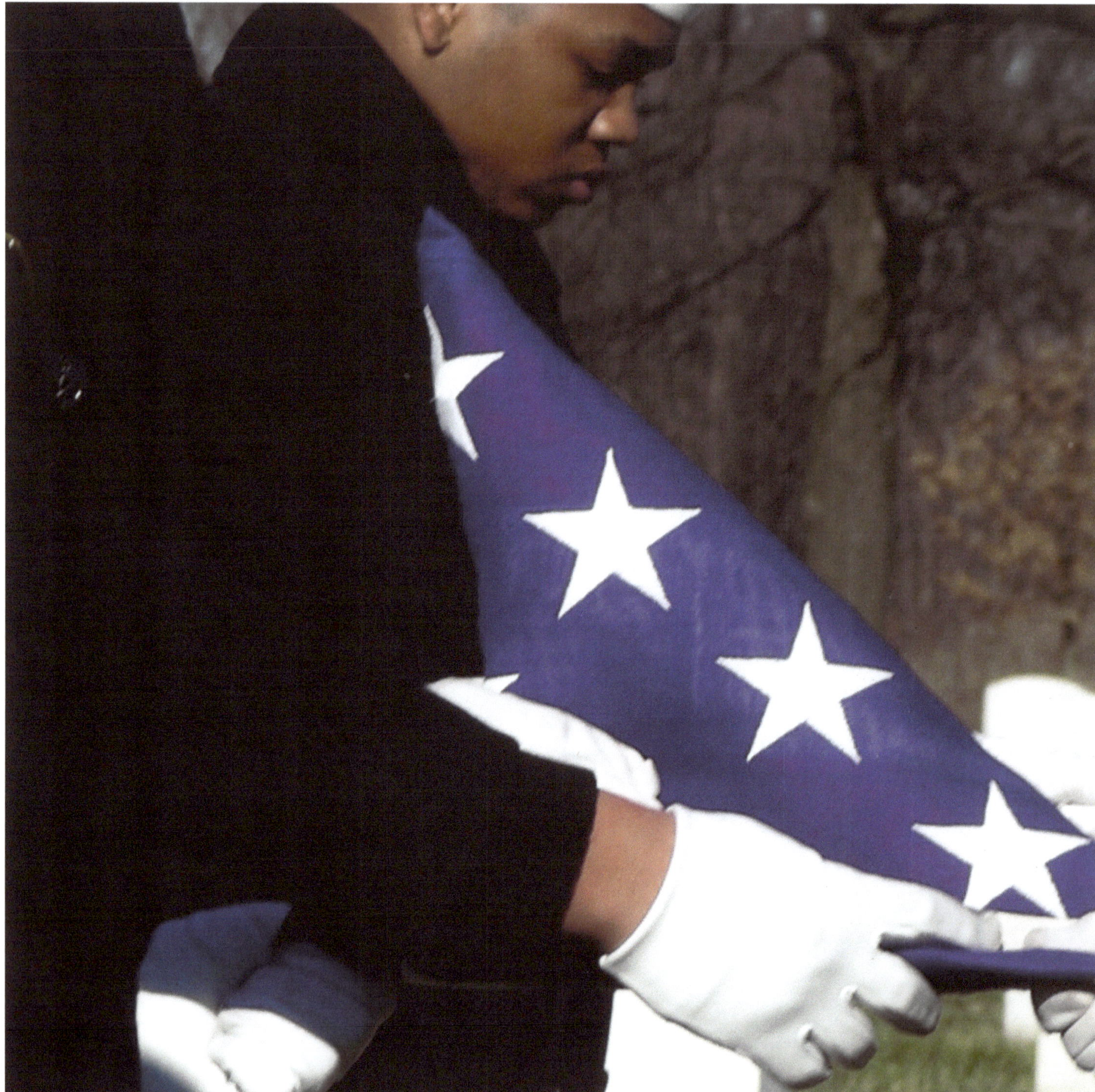

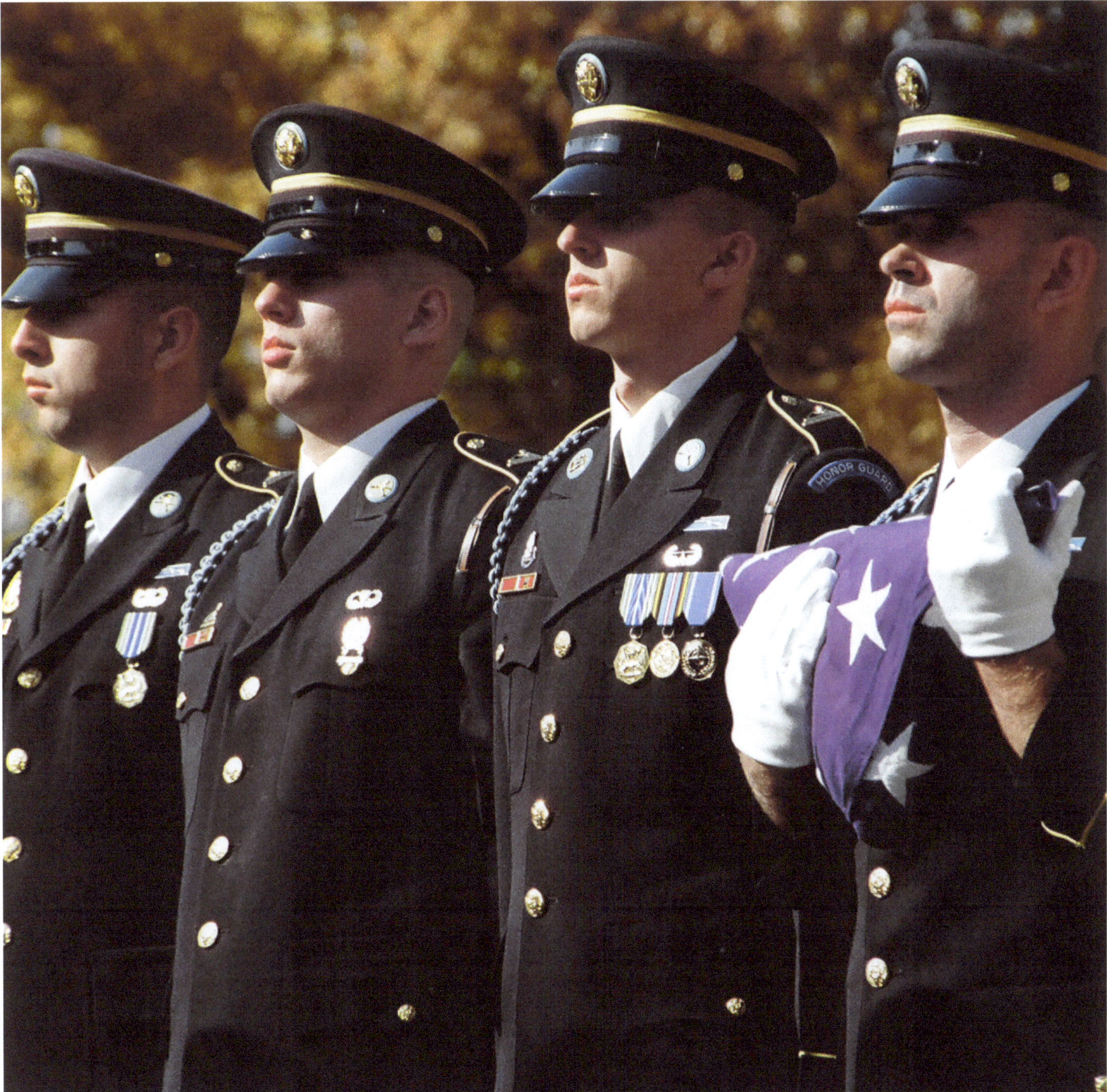
HONOR GUARD

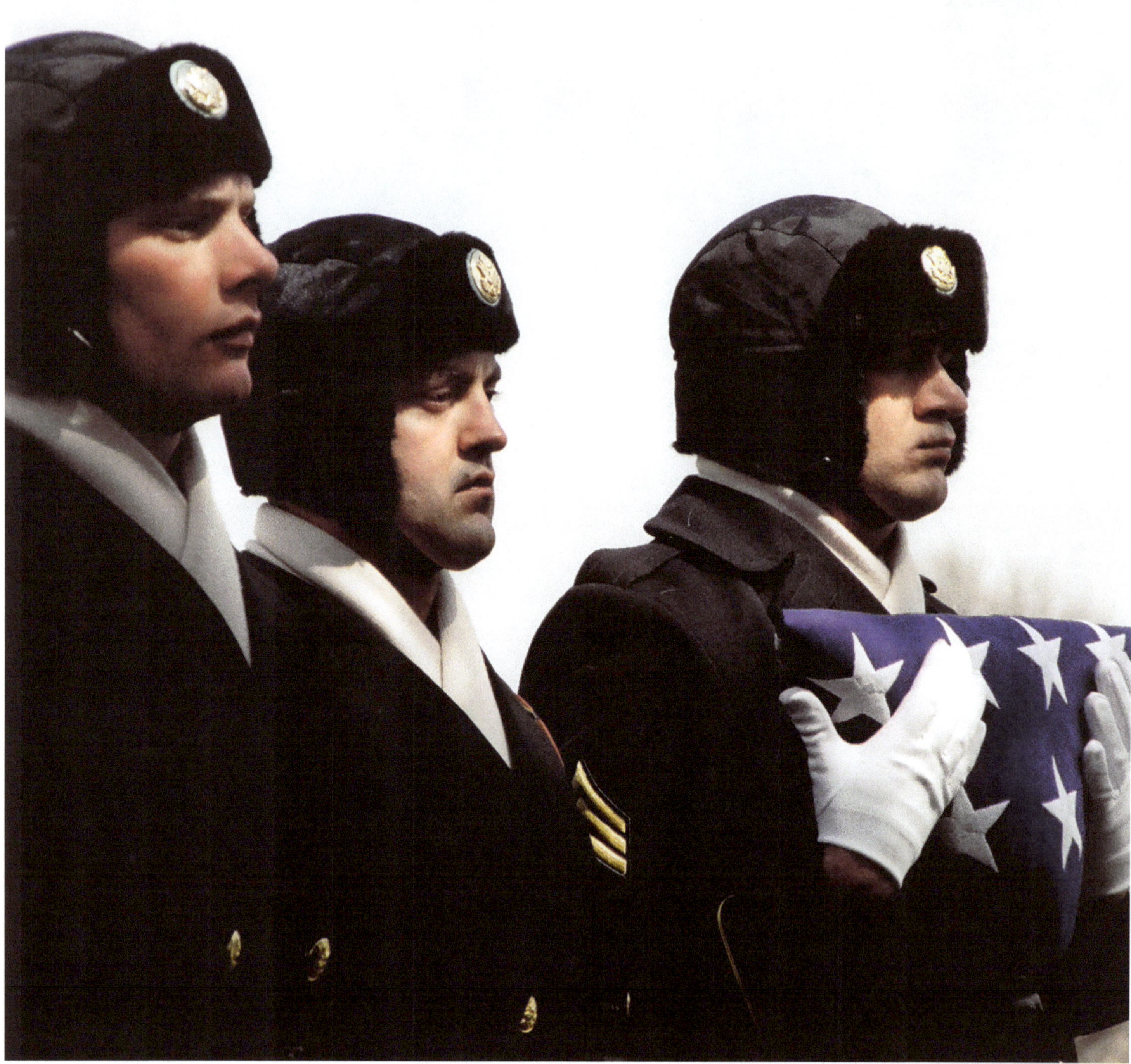

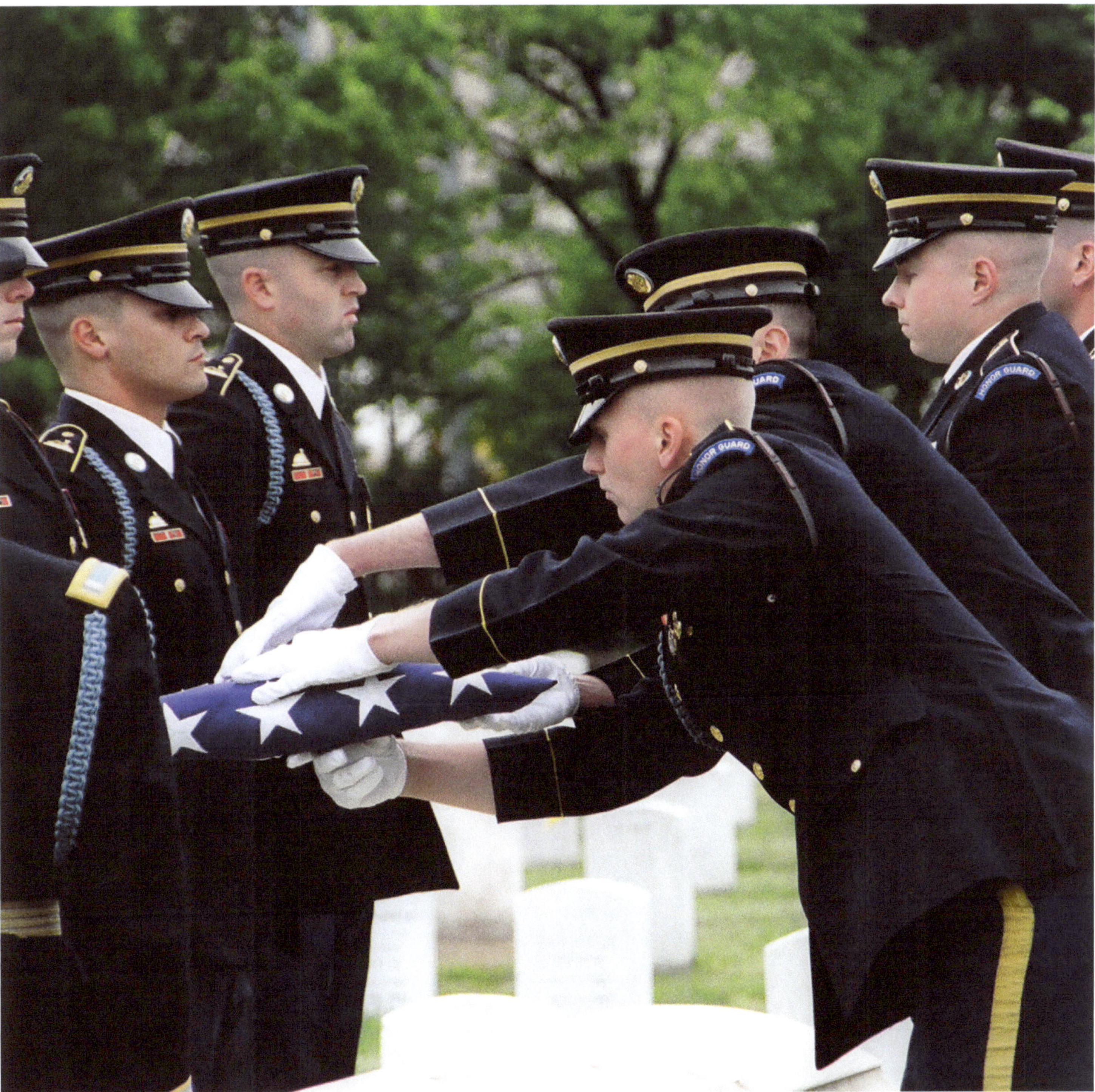
HONOR GUARD

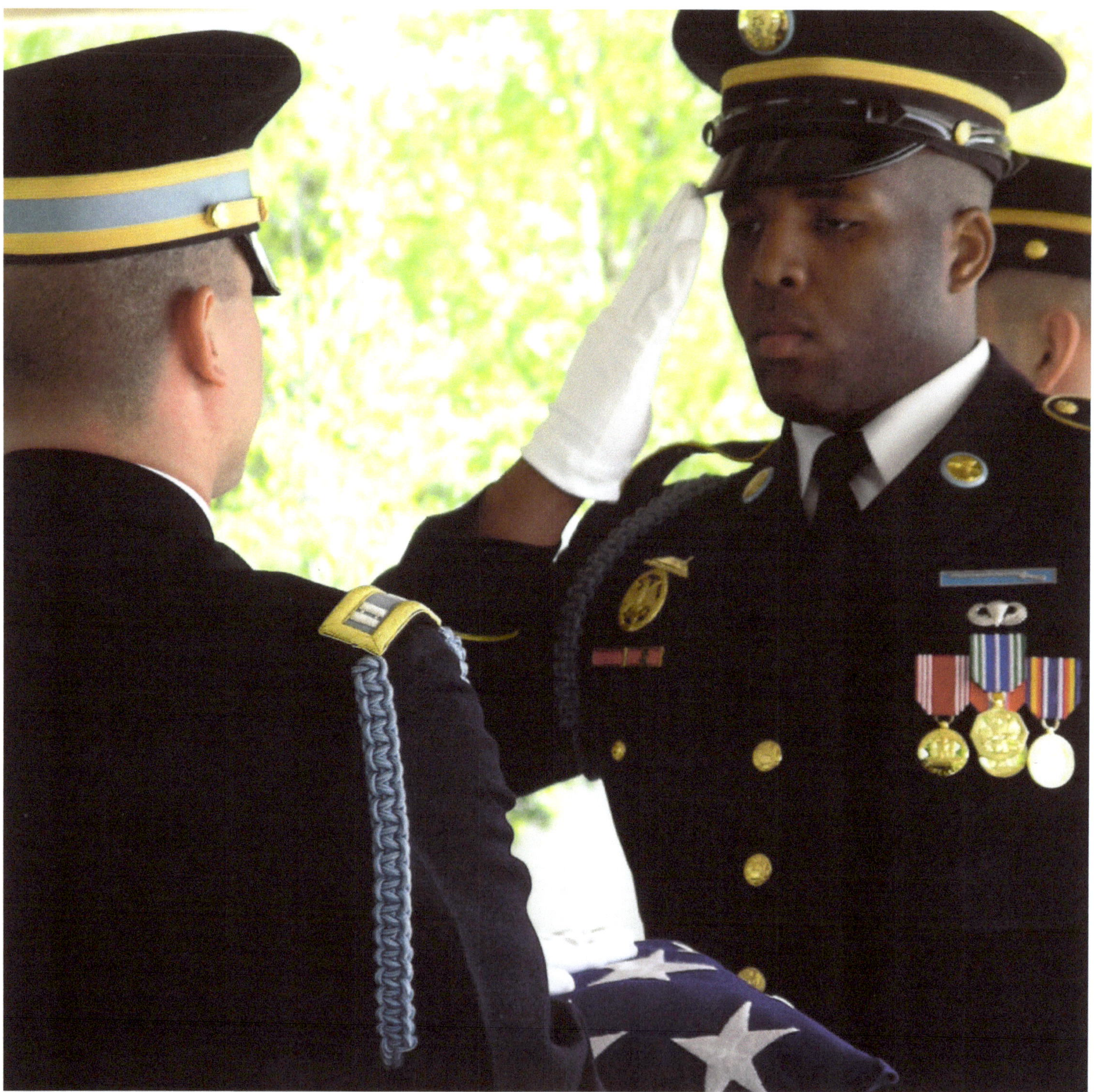

"On Behalf of a Grateful Nation..."

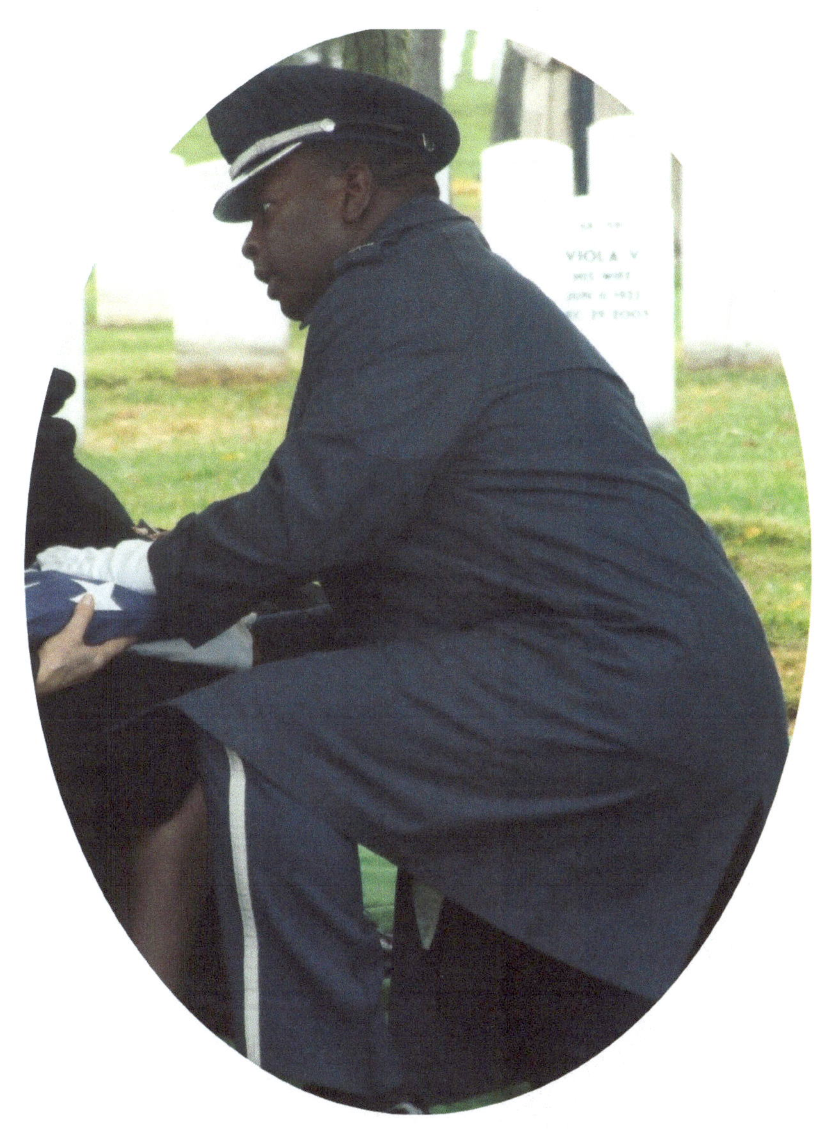

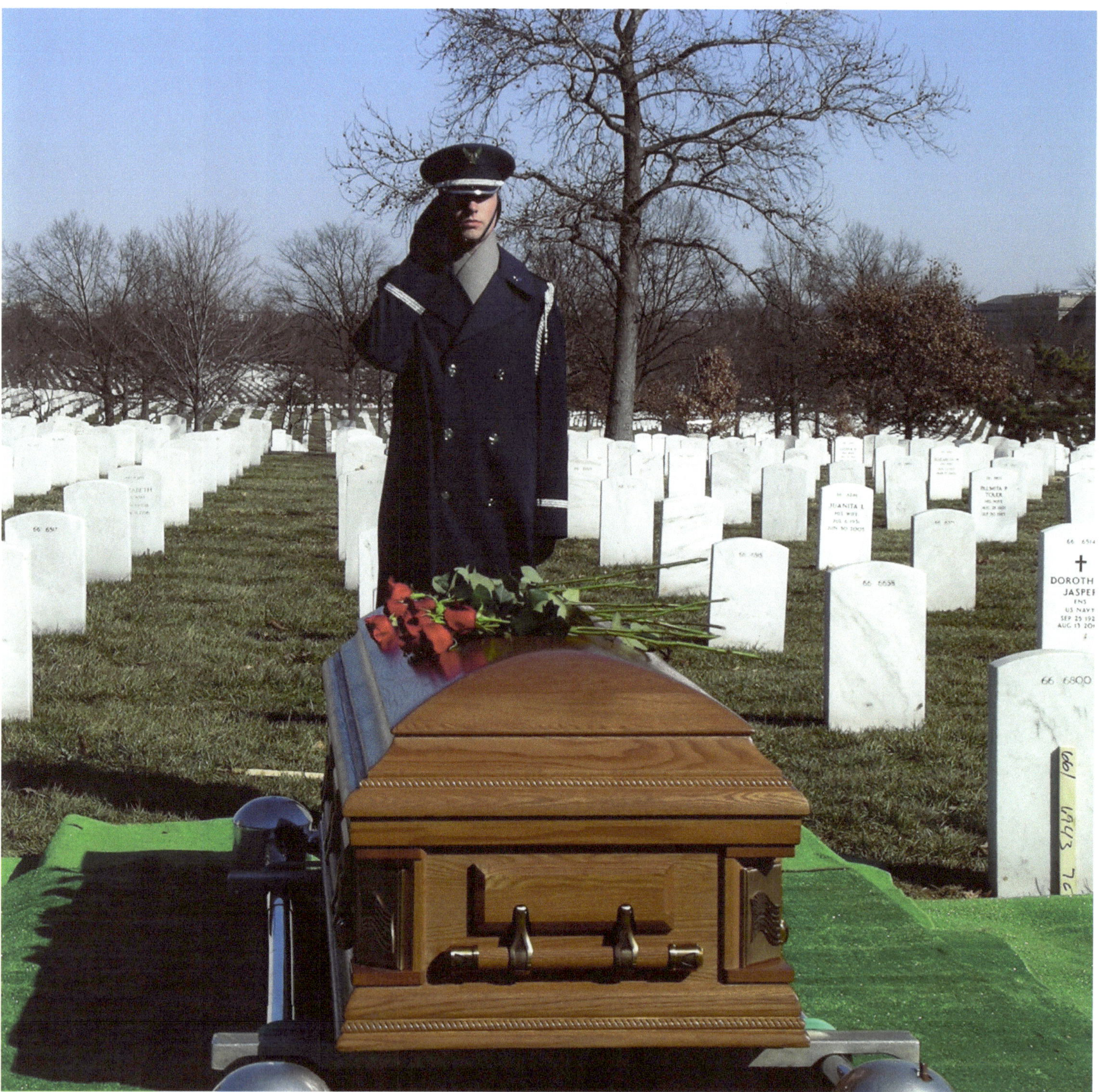
JUANITA L
HIS WIFE
JUN 30 2005
TOLER
66 6658
DOROTH
JASPER
ENS
US NAVY
66 6800

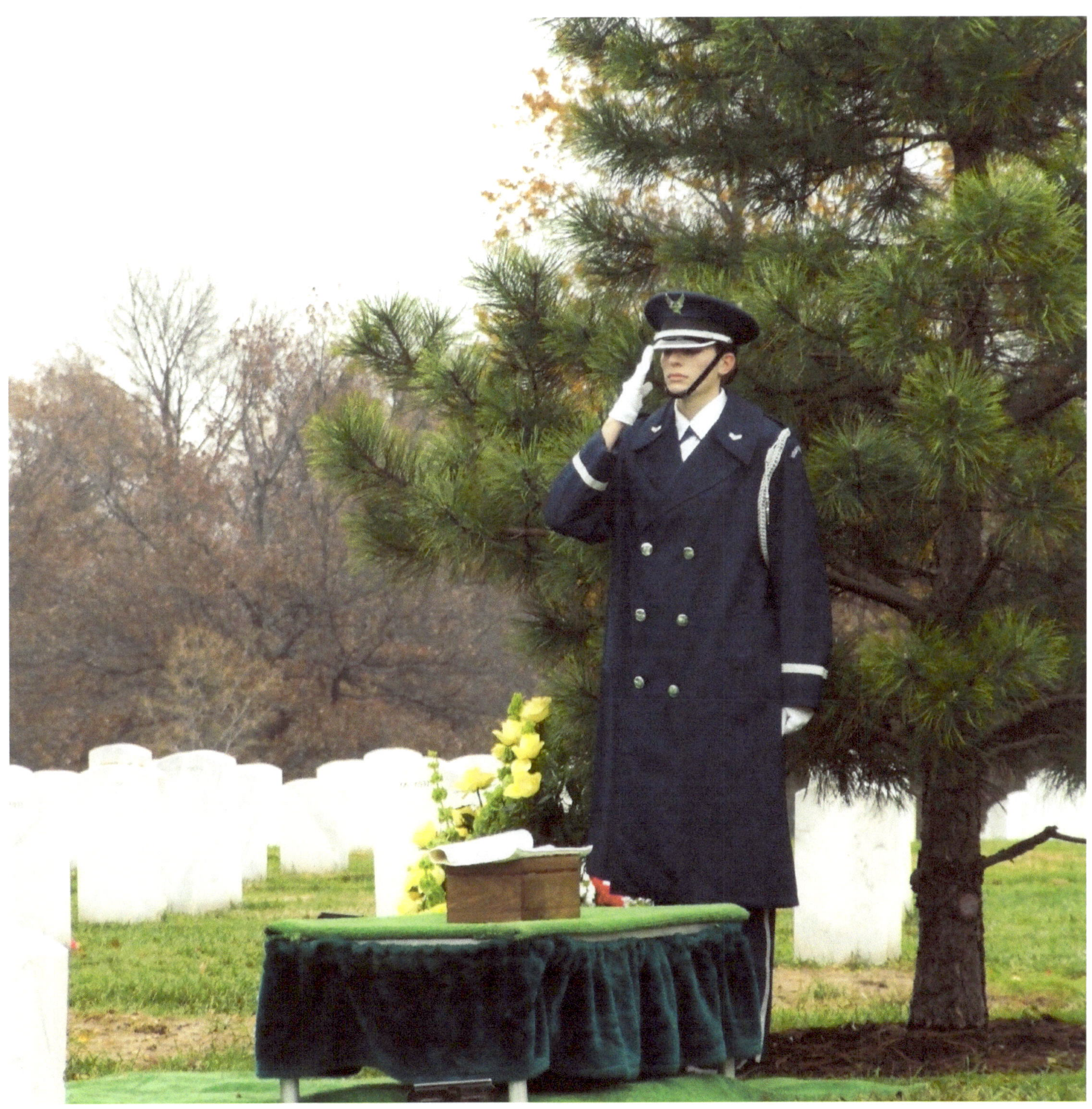

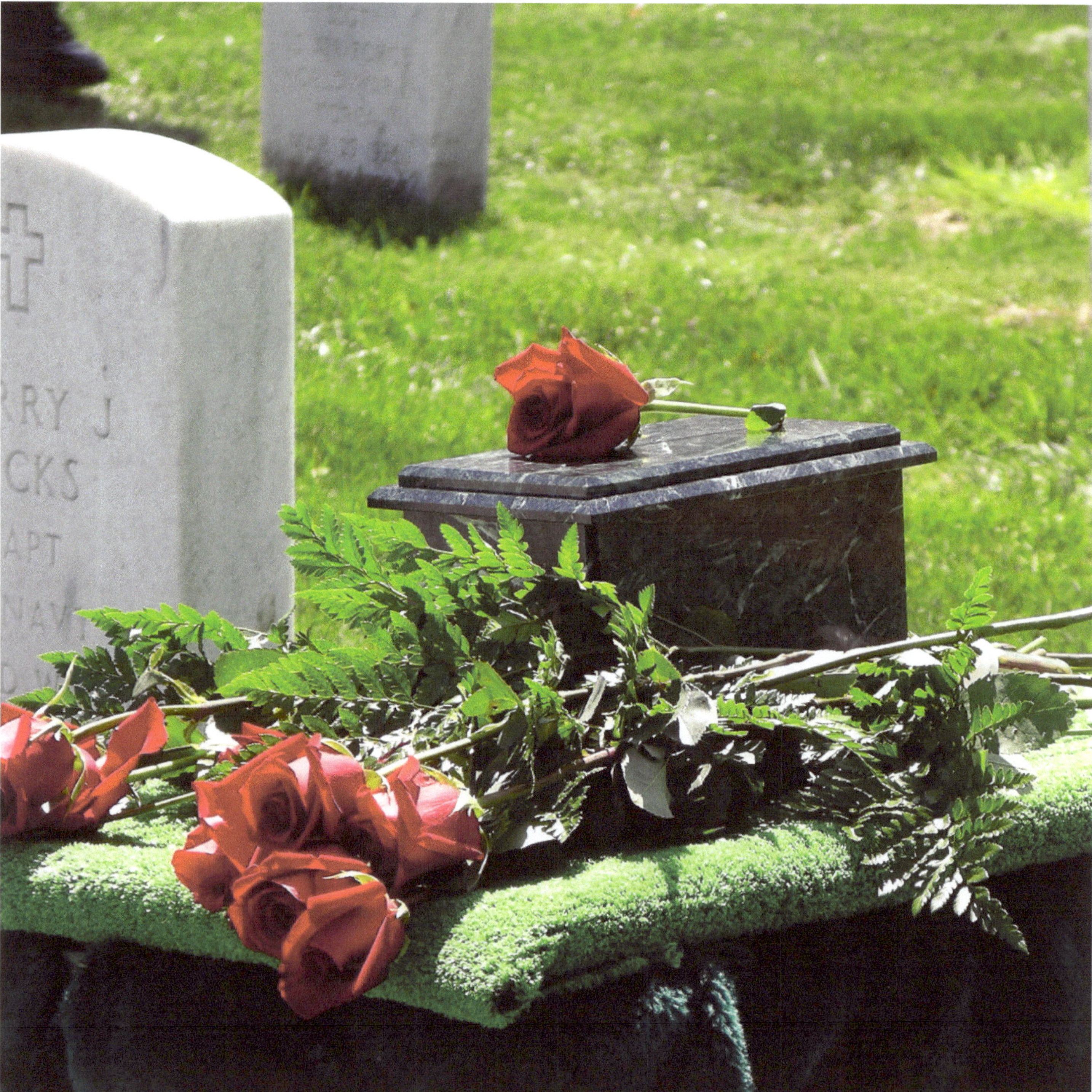
RRY J
CKS
APT

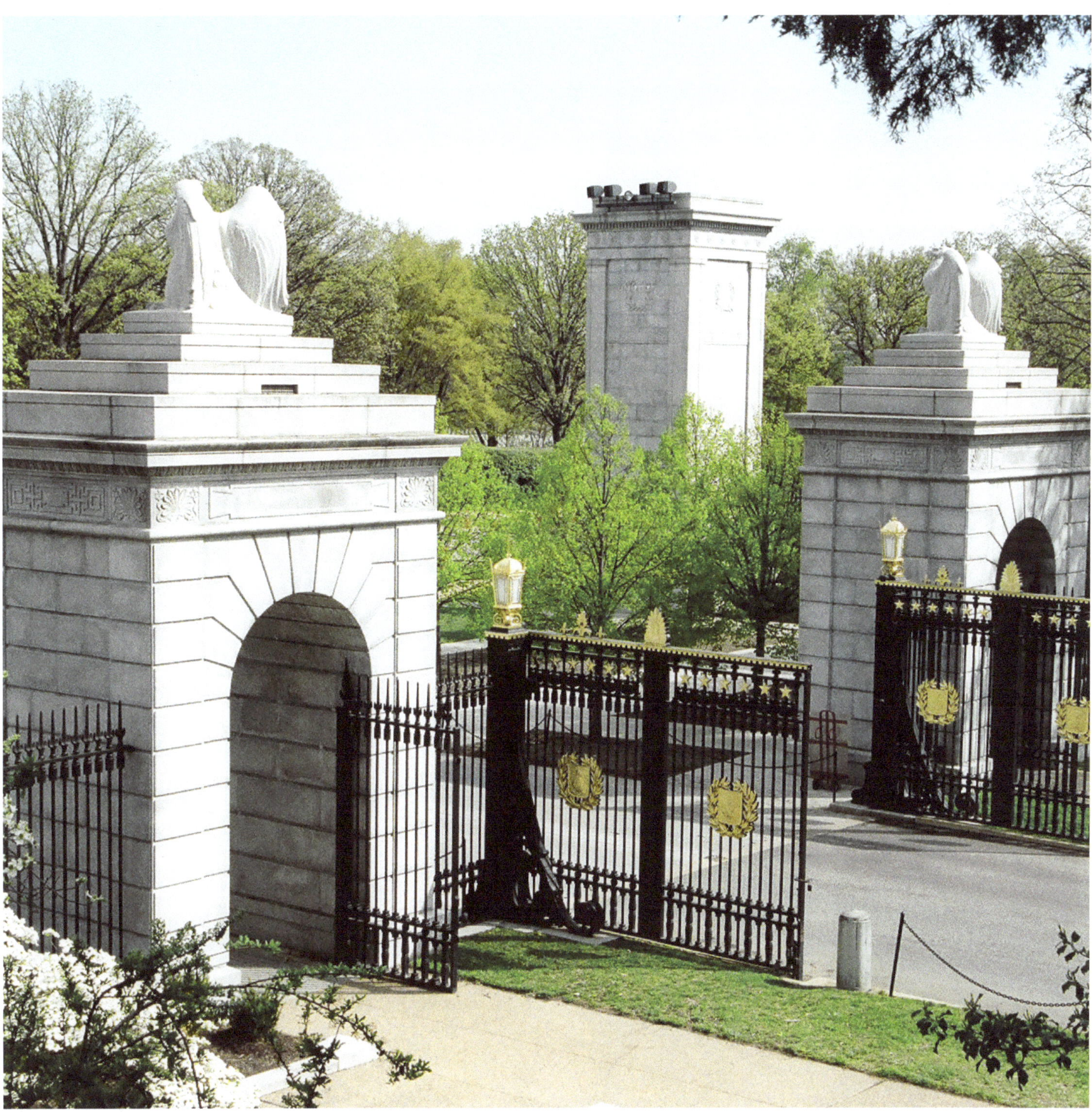

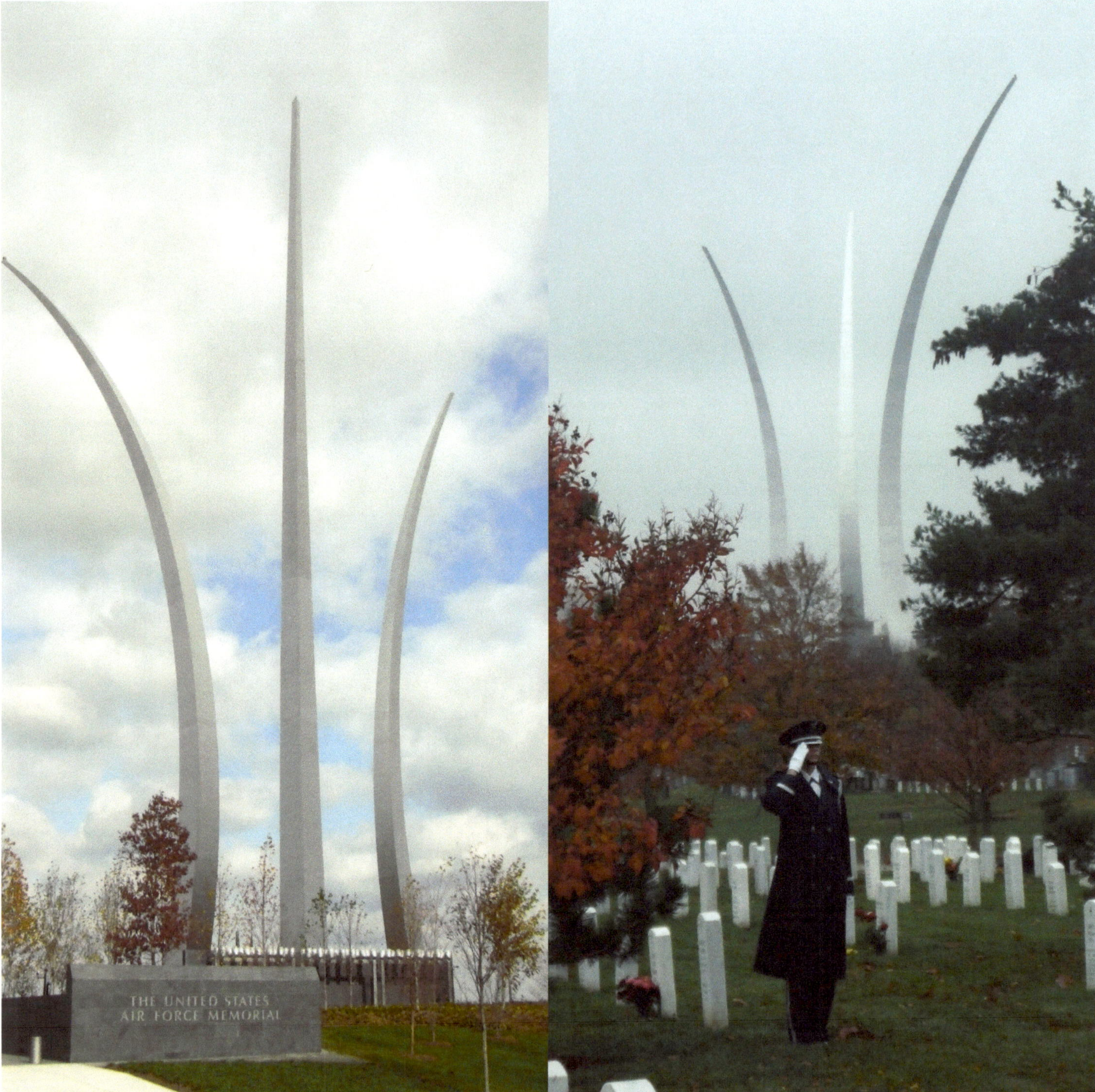
THE UNITED STATES
AIR FORCE MEMORIAL

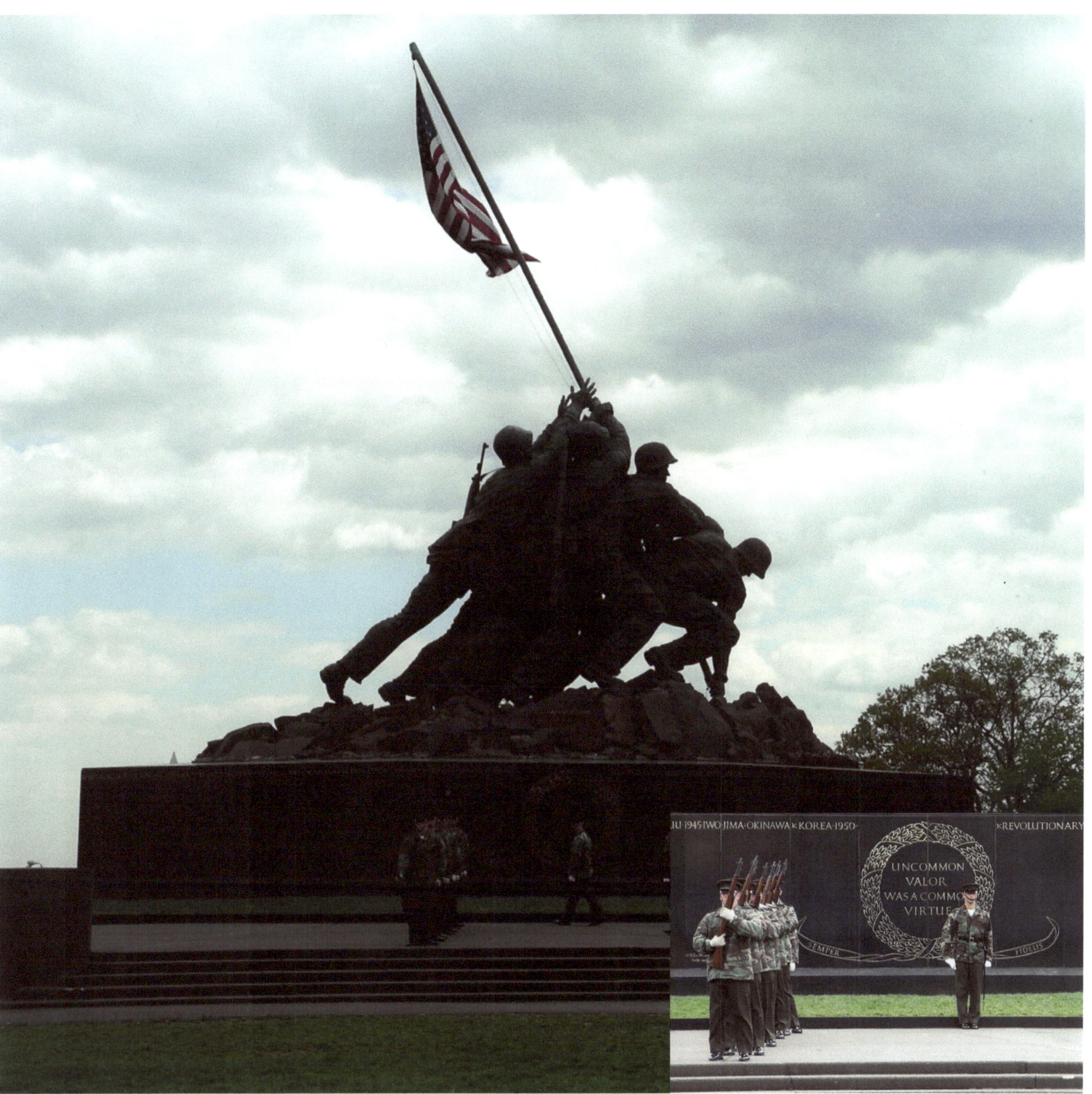
1945·IWO JIMA·OKINAWA
KOREA·1950
REVOLUTIONARY
UNCOMMON
VALOR
WAS A
VIRTUE
SEMPER
FIDELIS

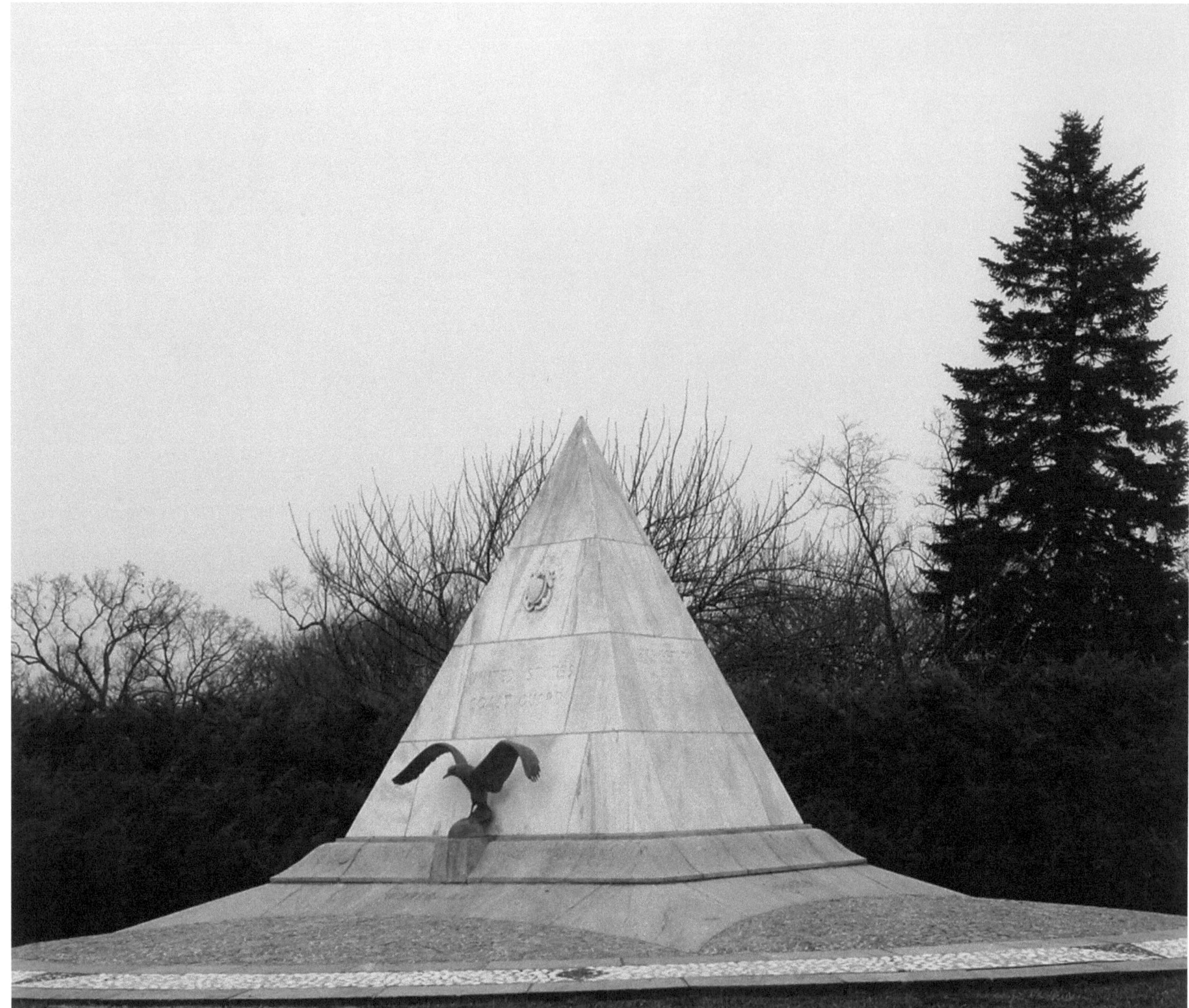
Coast Guard Memorial

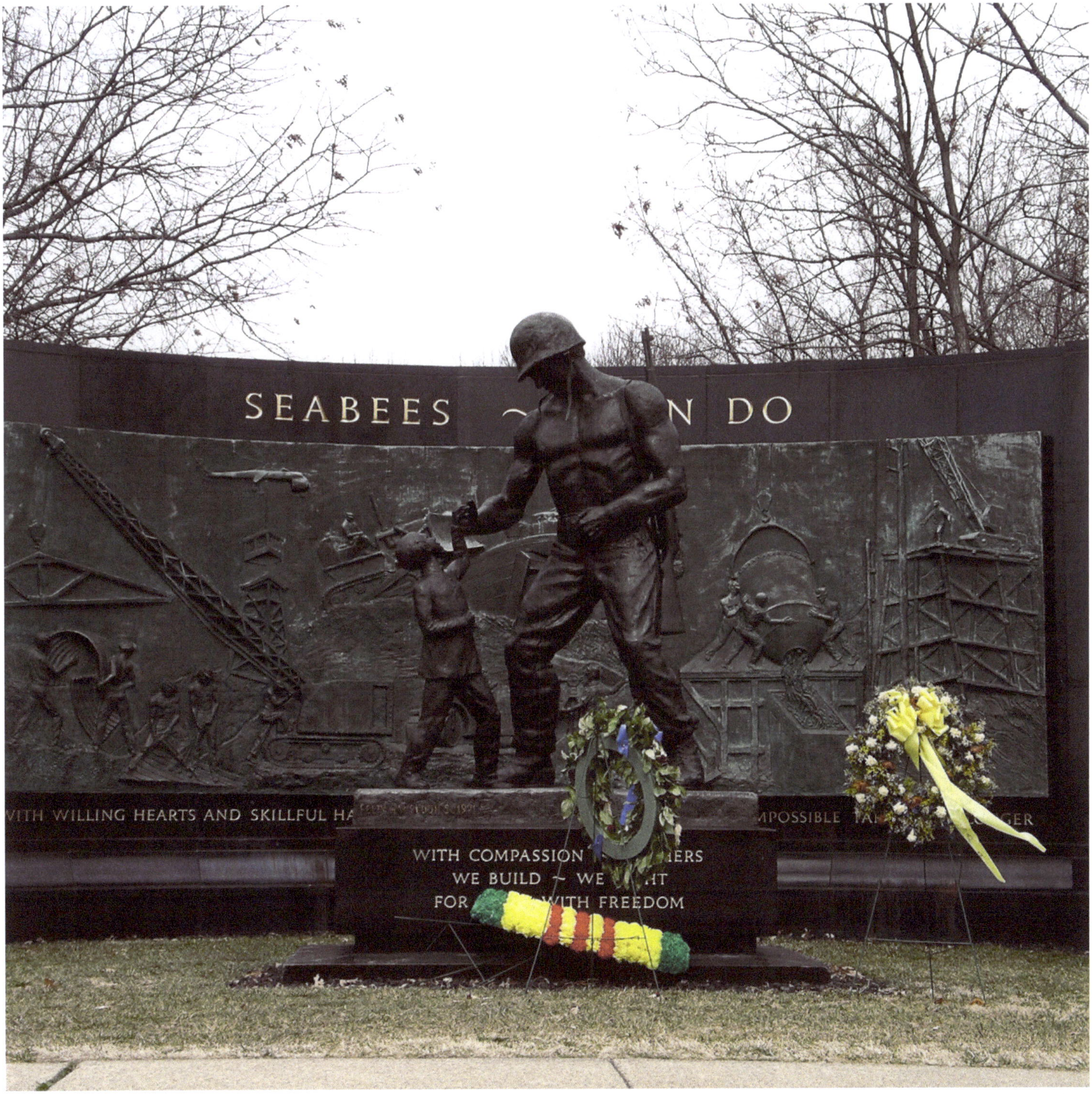

SEABEES
DO
WITH WILLING HEARTS AND SKILLFUL
WITH COMPASSION
WE BUILD ~ WE
WITH FREEDOM

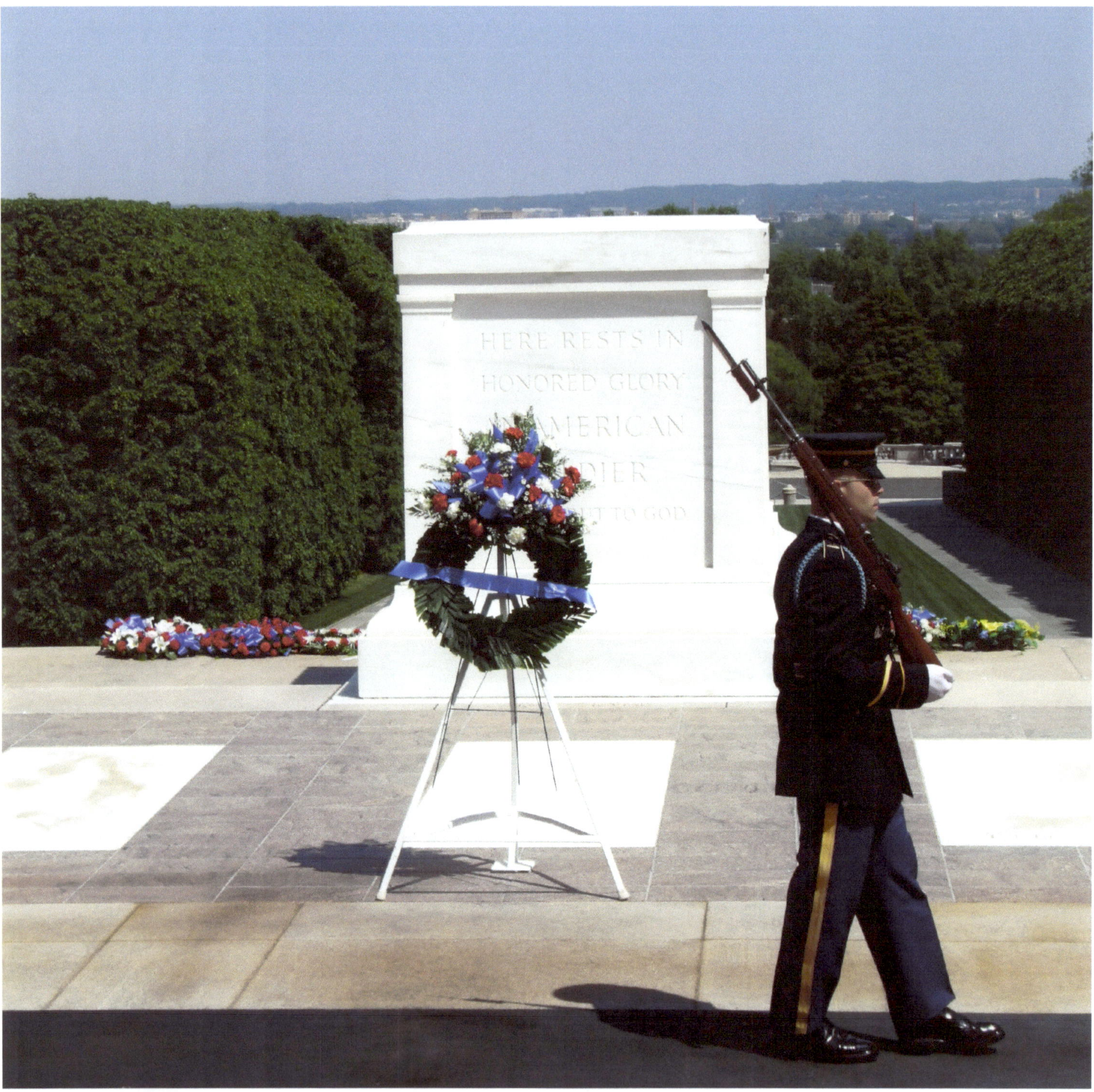
HERE RESTS IN
HONORED GLORY
AMERICAN

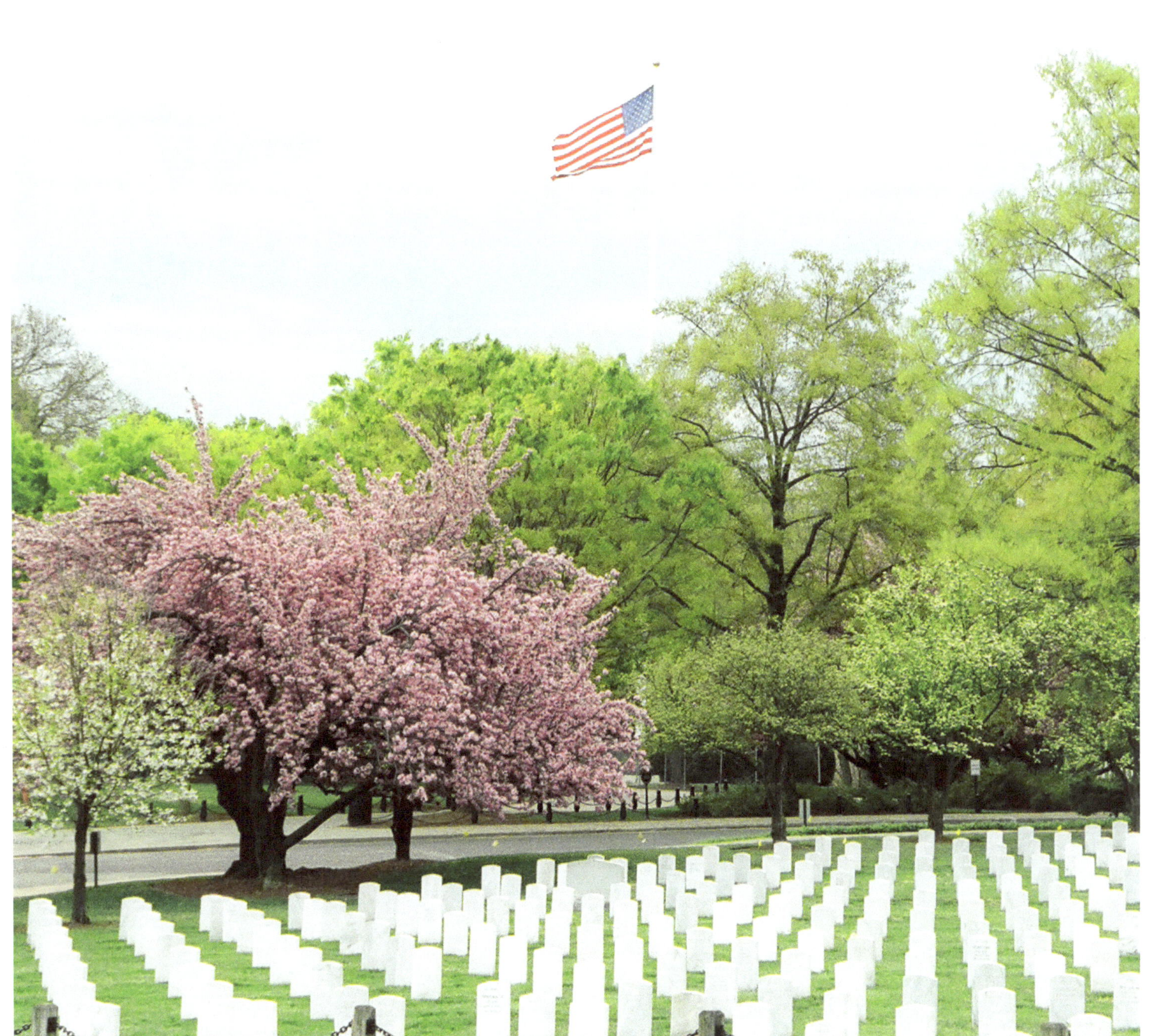

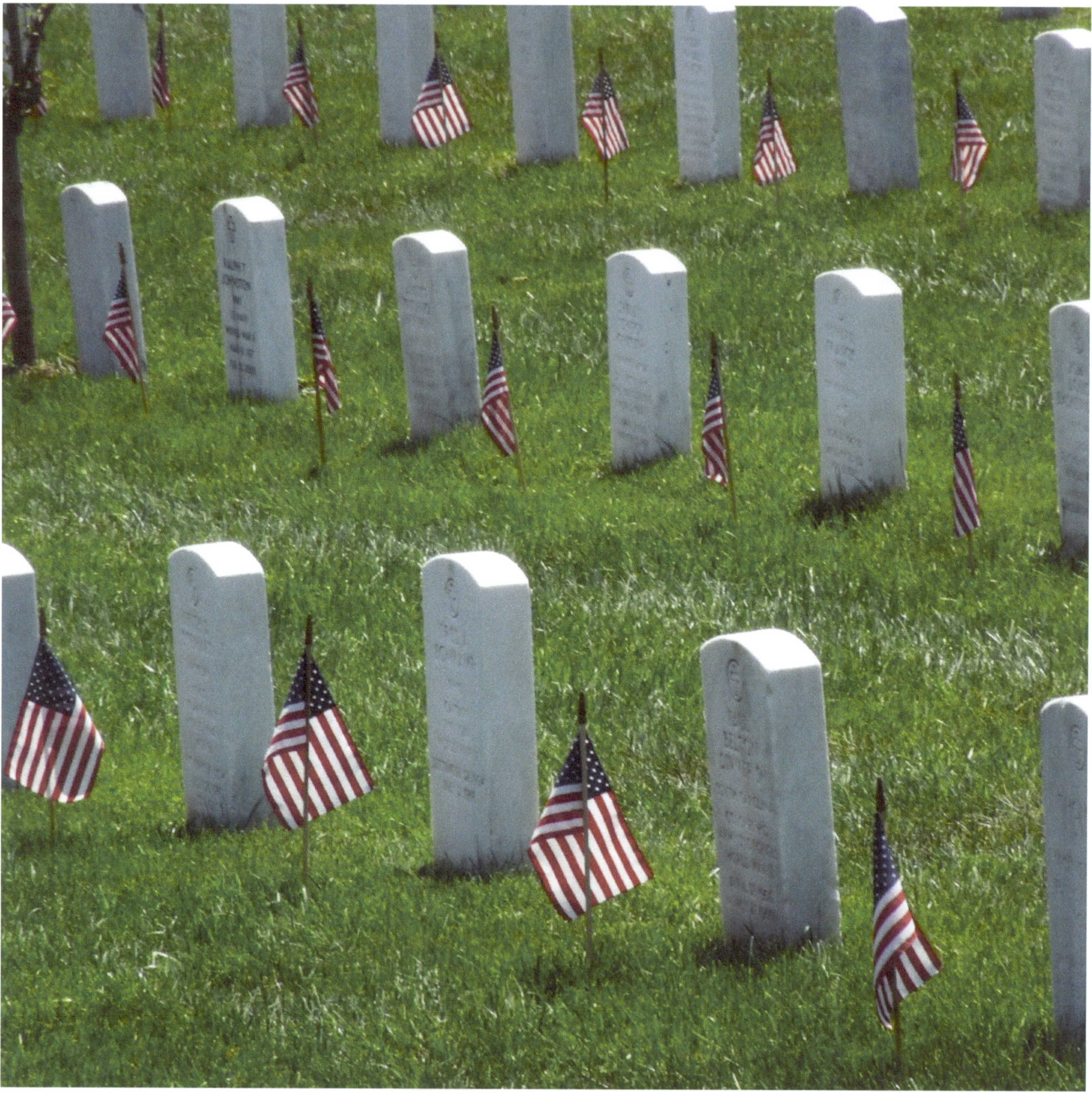

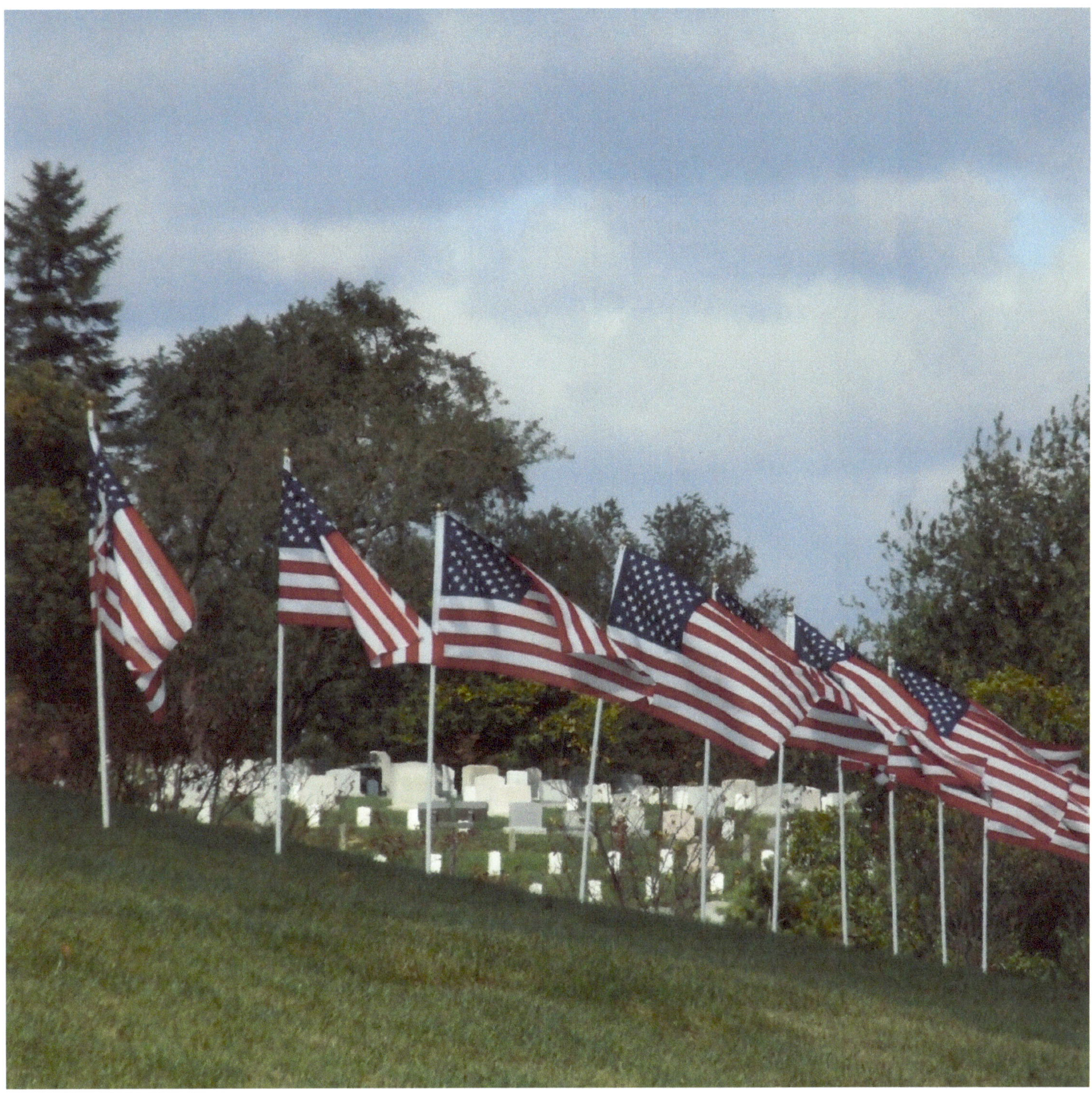

www.ingramcontent.com/pod-product-compliance
Lightning Source LLC
LaVergne TN
LVHW070146110826
845147LV00002B/332

* 9 7 8 0 6 1 5 1 5 2 4 4 8 *